LESSONS IN CHESS

GARRY KASPAROV
AND THE KASPAROV CHESS ACADEMY

EVERYMAN CHESS

First published in 1997 by Gloucester Publishers plc, (formerly Everyman Publishers plc), Northburgh House, 10 Northburgh Street, London, EC1V 0AT

Reprinted 2004

British Library Cataloguing-in-Publication Data
A catalogue record for this book is available from the British Library.

ISBN 1 85744 164 8

Distributed in North America by The Globe Pequot Press, P.O Box 480, 246 Goose Lane, Guilford, CT 06437-0480.

All other sales enquiries should be directed to Gloucester Publishers plc, Northburgh House, 10 Northburgh Street, London, EC1V 0AT
tel: 020 7253 7887 fax: 020 7490 3708
email: info@everymanchess.com
website: www.everymanchess.com

Everyman is the registered trade mark of Random House Inc. and is used in this work under license from Random House Inc.

EVERYMAN CHESS SERIES (formerly Cadogan Chess)

Chief Advisor: Garry Kasparov
Commissioning Editor: Byron Jacobs

Typeset by ChessSetter

Printed by Lightning Source

Contents

A Riddle of a Wise Man

For about two thousand years, people have tried to uncover the secrets of chess. In many respects it has long ceased to be a mystery. An orderly theory has been created to be used by millions of chess players for study and perfection of their skill, but just as hundreds of years ago they still roam the interminable labyrinth of the chessboard.

At all times there existed players who were regarded as the best in the world. They thought that they kept Ariadne's thread firmly in their hands and that it would lead them out of this labyrinth. But every time new heroes appeared and overthrew the former champions. Nobody remained undefeated for long.

Where did this wonderful game come from? Perhaps it was a present from our intelligent cosmic brothers? No, chess was invented by a human being. His name is unknown but his native land was India. Very long ago, at very outset of the Christian era, the game that later won millions of hearts all over the world made its triumphant start from this wonderland. Many beautiful legends are connected with the invention of chess. This is the most popular.

Long, long ago, a rajah by the name of Sheram ruled India. He felt bored in his luxurious palace, and once, in order to entertain him, his courtiers showed him a new game called chess. Sheram liked the game and wished to see the inventor. A Brahmin bent by old age came before his throne.

"Is it you who invented this wonderful game, wise man?" asked the rajah. "Ask for any reward. I'll not begrudge you anything."

"O, my sovereign! Your kindness is unbounded," answered the Brahmin, "but I only need bread. Order your servants to take a chessboard and put a wheat grain onto one of the squares."

"A wheat grain?" the rajah asked again, thinking that he not heard correctly.

"Yes, my sovereign. But order them to put two grains on the second square, four grains on the third square, eight grains on the fourth square and so on, every time doubling the number of grains."

"You will get your sack of grain!" answered the annoyed rajah, "but God knows that your choice is unworthy of my generosity. Be gone, my servants will bring you the grain."

The rajah called the court mathematicians and asked them to count the number of grains the silly Brahmin would have as a reward. There were no computers at that time and the process of calculation proved to be rather long.

Next day Sheram asked the senior mathematician whether the old man had got his meagre reward.

The mathematician answered with trepidation:

"O, my sovereign! This amount of grain cannot be found either in your rich granaries or indeed in the whole world..."

"What then is this incredible number?"

"O, my sovereign! It is eighteen quintillion, four hundred and forty-six quadrillion, seven hundred and forty-four trillion, seventy-three billion, seven hundred and nine million, five hundred and fifty-one thousand, six hundred and fifteen grains!"

Evidently, the Brahmin did not get his reward. To gather in such a harvest, one must sow eight times the whole surface area of the earth, and in order to store this amount of grain, one needs an elevator four meters high, ten meters wide and ... 300 million kilometres long, or twice the distance from the Earth to the Sun!

The inventor of chess was a wise man indeed. He provided his game with many properties that have made it immortal, namely the beauty of logic, the flight of fantasy, and boundless possibilities. He created a small model of life itself, with its joys and griefs, and gave it the form of a competition of intellects and personalities, touching the sensitive strain of human nature and the desire to measure oneself against a rival.

Chess is not only a fascinating game, it is also a test of will, endurance and skill. And whereas the secret of the eternal youth of chess is its inexhaustibility, the secret of skill is knowledge and experience.

To become a true expert, one has constantly to perfect one's skill. The seeming ease with which the eminent chess players of the world gain their splendid victories is not only due to their talent, but also the result of endless effort.

Everything starts at the beginning. There is no mathematics without the multiplication table, there is no figure skating without tuition. The same applies to chess: one cannot achieve success without mastering the fundamentals of theory and practice.

This is a small chess book, covering the fundamentals. It will serve as a lighthouse in the boundless ocean of chess, to help you boldly navigate your ship in stormy waters and lead you to the joy of creation and to success.

On the Bridge

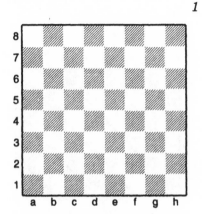

1

2

Here is a **board** divided into 64 **squares**, 32 light squares and 32 dark squares. This is the arena where the chess battle takes place, but do not hurry to set up the chessmen. Before starting a military action, you must learn to take your bearings on the board. Otherwise you will not know how to give orders and read reports from the battlefield.

The chessboard has its own geography. If a ship is wrecked in the open sea, the radioman sends a distress signal "SOS" and the geographic co-ordinates, the longitude and the latitude. The ships that go to its rescue seek the distressed ship in the region of intersection of these co-ordinates. The same principle is used to find any square on the chessboard.

The longitude is measured by eight vertical lines called files and denoted by the initial letters of the alphabet, i.e. a, b, c, d, e, f, g, h.

3

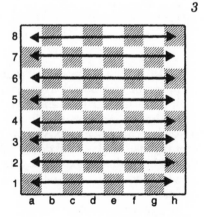

The latitude is measured by horizontal lines, from the first to the eighth, called ranks.

The e-file, for instance, embraces eight squares from e1 to e8 and the fourth rank embraces eight squares from a4 to h4.

Every square is located on a unique file and on a unique rank. Thus, each square is denoted by the letter of the file and the number of the rank at whose intersection it is located.

4

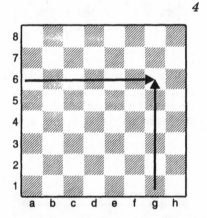

This is the notation of the squares of the board. Now you will not lose your way, and if you hear that your chessman is in distress on the g6-square, you will not run like mad up and down the board but will at once direct your naval glasses at the necessary point.

If you look attentively at the board, you are sure to notice there is a connection between squares of the same colour. All the squares of the same colour running in an inclined line are called **diagonals**.

5

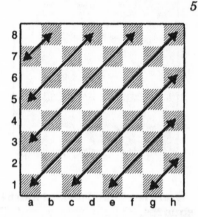

6

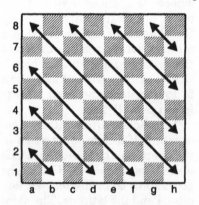

As opposed to ranks and files, diagonals vary in length. For instance, the a7-b8 diagonal consists of only two squares whereas the a3-f8 diagonal consists of six squares. The longest diagonals, extending from a1-h8 and h1-a8, consist of eight squares each. They are called **long diagonals**. There are **light-square** and **dark-square** diagonals.

7

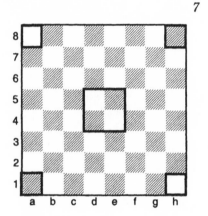

Groups of squares also have names. Four squares, namely, d4, e4, d5 and e5 are called **central squares** and together form the **centre** of the board. The **corner squares** are at a1, h1, a8 and h8 respectively.

The ability to take your bearings on the board makes it easy to calculate the variations and mentally see the arrangement of the chessmen, without setting them up on the board.

If you have learnt the fighting properties of chessmen and are able to visualise the chessboard, you will be able, in due course, to travel along it "blindfold". The former World Champion Alexander Alekhine was famous for playing without looking at the board.

"At high school," he recounted, "I got accustomed to play chess with the boy who sat at the same desk. Once the teacher caught us at it and took the chess set away. Then we decided to continue the game without the board and soon realised that it was much safer although less convenient..."

I hope that any young readers will not take this story as a recommendation to play chess during lessons!

Exercises

(1) Take a seat with your back to the chessboard. Let your friend ask you questions looking at *Diagram 4*. For instance, what is the colour of the f7-square? Which squares lie on the b-file? How many squares are there on the h4-d8 diagonal? Name them. Name all the squares that lie on the sixth rank. Then change places and let your friend answer your questions.

(2) You surely know the "Battleship Game". Draw the squares of a chessboard (8 x 8 squares) and the contours of ships in your notebook and begin a battle using chess notation. You must place your squadrons in a different position every time. Here is one possibility:

Lessons in Chess

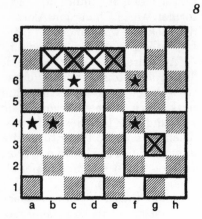

8

At first you will be slow, but soon you will be able to orientate on the board much better.

Rivals in White and Black

Two rivals participate in a chess battle. One of them commands the **white** pieces and the other commands the **black** pieces. Every army consists of sixteen warriors, namely, one **king**, one **queen**, two **rooks**, two **bishops**, two **knights** and eight **pawns**. Each chessman is denoted by a special symbol.

King	K	♚
Queen	Q	♛
Rook	R	♜
Bishop	B	♝
Knight	N	♞
Pawn	P	♟

In this book we will use the graphic symbols in the right-hand column above, but some books use letters instead of symbols. However, the pieces have different names in different languages. For instance, a bishop is called an 'elephant' in Russian, a 'runner' in German, a 'joker' in French, an 'archer' in Czech, and an 'officer' in Bulgarian. The letters used for the pieces therefore vary from language to language; the English letters are given in the middle column above. However, the symbols are always the same, whatever the language.

In the starting position White's and Black's pieces stand facing each other in a definite order.

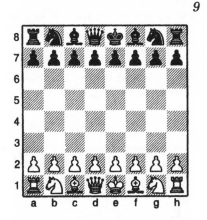

9

In chess **diagrams** (graphical representations of the board) it is customary to place the white chessmen in the lower part and the black men in the upper part of the board. You can see from the above diagram that the white and black men are represented differently.

The ranks are counted upwards and the files from left to right viewed from the white side.

Remember that **the board has to be set up so that the corner square on the right of each**

player is white ('white on the right' is easy to remember).

Do not misplace the queen and the king. In the starting position the white queen is always on the white square (d1) and the black one on the black square (d8). It is easy to remember this with the rule **the queen prefers its own colour**. As to the kings, they are capricious and do the opposite. Let us get acquainted with some other terms used in chess literature.

Suppose we draw an imaginary line between the fourth and the fifth rank.

10

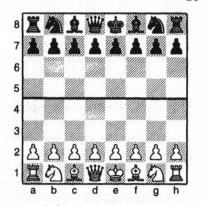

This is something like a state frontier. The upper half is the camp of Black **(Black's side)** and the lower half is the camp of White **(White's side)**.

Let us now draw a similar line between the files "d" and "e".

11

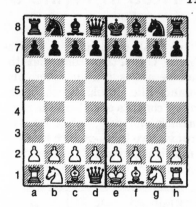

We have again divided the board into two equal parts. The half of the board containing both kings is called the **kingside** and that which contains both queens is called the **queenside**.

Although all the pawns look identical, we give them the names of the pieces in front of which they start. Therefore we distinguish between **rook's**, **knight's**, **bishop's**, **queen's** and **king's** pawns. You will learn later on that every pawn has its peculiarities.

We distinguish the following pairs of pieces on each side in the starting position. We call the kingside pieces the **king's bishop**, **king's knight** and **king's rook**; the queenside pieces are called the **queen's bishop**, **queen's knight** and **queen's rook**.

Thus we have set up pieces and pawns in fighting order, the forces on both sides being equal in number. What is the difference between the white and the black pieces? The difference is that according to the laws **the game is always started by White**. Thus White is always one move ahead. When beginners play, it is usually of no importance, but with experienced players it sometimes proves to be a serious advantage.

Once the famous Russian chess player Mikhail Chigorin was asked whether the choice of a colour was of any importance for him. "Of no importance", he joked. "I win when I play White because I start and I win when I play Black because I am Chigorin!" (*Editor's note*: This saying is usually attributed to Chigorin).

The colour taken by the players in tournaments is determined by special regulations. In a casual game it is better for you to draw lots before the game, in order to decide who plays White. It is reasonable that in consecutive games the players take turns playing White.

The two players move alternately. Two consecutive moves by the same player are prohibited, and a player is forbidden to pass his turn. **If you touch one of your men, you must move it; if you touch one of your opponent's men, you must take it**.

The "touch-move" rule is the main rule of behaviour in playing chess. If you want to adjust a chessman untidily placed, you must warn your opponent by saying: "j'adoube" ("I adjust").

Unfortunately, not only beginners sometimes feel tempted to change a move that has proved to be a poor one. Once, taking part in an international tournament, the Yugoslav Grandmaster Milan Matulović, in a game against the Hungarian Grandmaster Istvan Bilek, touched a piece but then changed his mind and moved another piece. Bilek was so taken aback that he made a protest only when the game was finished. All the participants denounced Matulović's action.

"I said 'j'adoube' but my opponent did not hear what I said", the Yugoslav tried to justify himself.

Nobody could prove or refute this statement, but when, before the next game, Matulović complained of a sore throat to the tournament doctor, the latter could not resist the temptation to say "I am afraid that the words 'j'adoube' have stuck in your throat...".

Because of this incident Matulovic got an offensive but well-deserved nickname "Grandmaster J'adoubović".

Exercises

(3) The position of White at the start is written as ♔e1, ♕d1, ♖a1, ♖h1, ♗c1, ♗f1, ♘b1, ♘g1, ♙a2, b2, c2, d2, e2, f2, g2, h2. Write down the position of Black.

Lessons in Chess

(4) Without looking at the board, specify which squares are occupied by Black's king's bishop, White's queen's rook, Black's king's knight and finally White's bishop's pawns.

Chessmen on Parade

The game of chess is based on the interaction of all the pieces. It is hard for a chessman to fight alone, the pieces must help one another. As in real life, on the chessboard only mutual aid and support lead to success. Do you remember the motto of the Three Musketeers? – "One for all and all for one!" Since the chessmen differ in their ability for long-range shooting and obey different rules of movement, each of them has its own speciality. In this sense, chess can be compared to an experienced football team in which each player is specialised in shooting from some particular spot of the penalty area.

You must know the behaviour of the chessmen in order not to find yourself in a situation like the following one.

Once the World Champion José Raoul Capablanca gave a simultaneous display.

"What do you think of my performance?" a young man asked him after the game.

"Not bad", Capablanca replied politely, "but why didn't you move your knights?"

"But I don't know how they move", the "chess player" admitted.

In this chapter you will find the laws according to which the pieces move on the board. Their possible moves are shown by arrows.

The King

Sixteen pieces and pawns take part in a chess battle on each side. All of them are useful and must not be wasted, but the most important piece is the king. Losing a piece does not mean the end of the game, except if the piece happens to be the king. If the king perishes, the game is lost.

The main goal in chess is to put the opponent in a position in which capture of the king is unavoidable, i.e. **to checkmate the king**. The word "check" (shah) is the Persian for "king" and "mate" is the Arabic for "dead". "The king is dead" means that the war is over. The winner is the player who first conquers the enemy king.

"I will checkmate you in three moves!" a certain hot-tempered Spaniard once exclaimed when he played against Alexander Alekhine.

"Don't worry, señor," the World Champion smiled, "I will checkmate you in two moves..."

But it is not so easy to capture the enemy king. The opponent's whole army defends it, and the piece itself, despite being rather slow, is very agile.

12

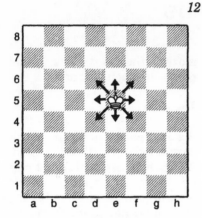

13

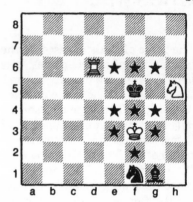

The king moves to an adjacent square in any direction and captures enemy men in the same way as it moves, if they are bold enough to come close to it without any protection. But the chess king is not all-powerful. The rules of the game forbid it to move to a square that is within the capturing range of an enemy piece. Therefore the king can never directly attack the enemy queen, which can act in all directions, nor can the two kings attack each other. As to the other pieces, the king, as a skilful hunter, steals up to them from the "lee side", i.e. from the squares that they cannot defend.

The squares to which the kings cannot move are marked with stars. These squares are under the fire of enemy pieces with which you will get acquainted later. On vacant squares the kings can indulge in hand-to-hand combat. For instance, after the move to g2 the white king attacks both the bishop and the knight. In its turn, the black king can attack the rook by making the move ...♔e5, or the knight by playing ...♔g5.

The Queen

The queen is the most powerful and the most mobile piece, the main attacking force of the chess army.

The queen can move in all directions along ranks, files and diagonals. It controls more squares than any other piece, 27 from the centre and 21 from a corner square.

Wherever it is, it can get to any empty square in no more than two moves, provided there are no obstructing pieces, and in different

14

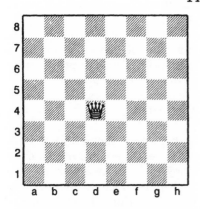

15

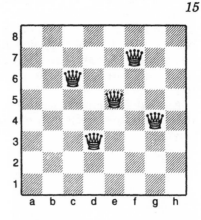

ways at that. For instance, in the diagram above the queen on d4 has to get to the h1-square. Here are the possible ways of doing this:

(1) ♕d4-d1-h1, (2) ♕d4-g1-h1, (3) ♕d4-h4-h1, (4) ♕d4-h8-h1, (5) ♕d4-a1-h1, (6) ♕d4-d5-h1, (7) ♕d4-e4-h1.

Five queens can control all the 64 squares of the chessboard. There are 4860 positions of this kind. Diagram 15 shows one.

Try to find some more positions of this type.

The Rook

The rook is a long-range piece but it can move only in a straight line. It moves along all the ranks and files backwards and forwards, to the right and to the left, from one edge of the board to the other. The rook can be compared to a ram which can breach a wall of the enemy fortress. It cannot move diagonally.

16

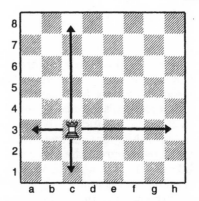

In the same way as the other pieces (except for the knight), the rook controls every square within its fighting range. For instance, White can move the rook not only to c8 or h3 but also to c7 or d3, in other words the rook may stop at any point of its route. On a board free from other pieces the rook controls 14 squares.

And what happens when the rook encounters an obstacle on its way?

17

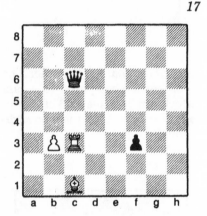

None of the pieces (except for the knight) can jump over other pieces, its own or hostile ones.

If a piece of the rook's colour is in its way, it hinders the movement of the rook. For instance, in the above diagram the squares a3, b3 and c1 are among those inaccessible for the rook.

If the obstructing unit is an enemy piece, the rook can take it, i.e. remove it from the board and occupy its place. In our example the rook has a choice of captures,

it can capture either the black queen on c6 or the black pawn on f3.

The rule of capturing is the same for all pieces. Every piece (except for pawns) captures in the same manner as it moves.

The Bishop

Bishops move along diagonals. As we already know, every chess army includes two bishops. One of them is on a light square in the initial position (f1 for White and c8 for Black) and is therefore called a light-squared bishop, the other is on a dark square (c1 and f8) and is called a dark-squared bishop. They can only move along the diagonals of their own colour. The paths of two bishops moving on different coloured squares never intersect; thus each bishop is able to control only half the board, either the 32 light squares or the 32 dark squares.

In the diagram on the next page White has a light-squared bishop and Black has a dark-squared bishop. After ♗d5-g8 the bishops stand side by side but they seem not to notice each other.

The mobility of this piece depends on its position on the chessboard. The white bishop on d5 can move to any one of 13 squares whereas its black opponent on f8 can move to only 7 squares. Conclusion: **pieces at the centre of**

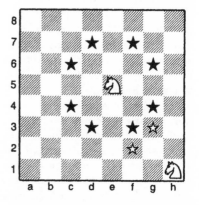

18

the board have greater free-
dom of movement.

How does this affect their fighting ability?

knight on f7 or the rook on g2.
The black bishop posted on the
edge of the board can attack only
two men, the pawn on b4 and the
rook on h6. It is clear which of the
bishops has the greater fighting
value!

The Knight

The knight moves in a peculiar
way which is not so easy to explain. Most of all its movement
resembles the letter L. Since the
letter sometimes comes up topsy-
turvy or upside-down, it is better
to illustrate the movement of the
knight by a diagram.

20

19

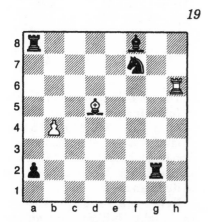

The white bishop posted at the
centre can attack four enemy men
simultaneously. It can take the
pawn on a2, the rook on a8, the

Suppose the e5-square, which
is occupied by one of the white
knights, is the centre of a circle,
the radius being the distance
from e5 to f7. The circle passes
through the centre of exactly

eight squares: f7, g6, g4, f3, d3, c4, c6 and d7.

The sphere of activity of the knight at the centre of the board resembles an open fan.

Pay attention to the fact that after each of these moves the knight jumps from a dark square to a light one.

The second knight is on the light square h1. It controls only the dark squares f2 and g3.

Conclusion: **after every move the knight changes the colour of the square it stands on.**

As distinct from the other chess pieces, the knight cannot stop its move half-way, it must complete its jump.

There are many fascinating mathematical problems involving the move of the knight. For instance, you may be asked to go all round the board stopping at every square only once. It is hard to believe that there are 30 million tours of this kind!

No other piece, placed on a corner square, loses its mobility to such an extent as the knight. Look at the diagram on the previous page and compare the manoeuvring ability of the two knights. The knight on h1 controls only two squares, i.e. a quarter of the squares controlled by the knight on e5. Therefore the strength of the knight increases as it moves to the centre. This peculiarity of the knight has great practical importance.

The knight possesses an important quality that distinguishes it from its fellow warriors. Any other piece moves only along empty lines; if it encounters another piece on its way, it cannot jump over it. As to the knight, there are no obstacles for it, it overcomes all barriers, whether its own men or the opponent's.

21

The white knight can make one of following moves at its choice: ♘d4-c2, ♘d4-b3, ♘d4-b5, ♘d4-c6, ♘d4-e6, ♘d4-f5, ♘d4-f3, ♘d4-e2. The black knight on d5 can make similar jumps. Find its moves and write them down.

Here is one more peculiarity of the knight. Unlike the queen, the rook and the bishop, the knight does not attack enemy pieces that are in its way. It jumps over them and can capture an enemy piece only on its destination square.

22

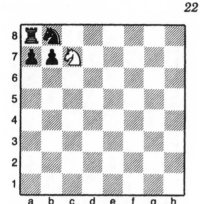

23

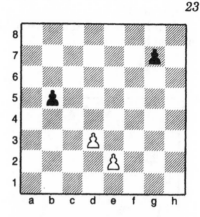

The white knight attacks the rook on a8, while the black knight on b8 and the pawns on a7 and on b7, over which it jumps, remain unharmed.

The Pawn

The pawn is the smallest of the pieces, a soldier in the chess army. Pieces can attack and retreat but a pawn knows only one command: "Forward!" It perishes but never flees from the battlefield.

A pawn can move only slowly, one square at a time. **Only at the first move can a pawn advance two squares.**

White can move his pawn from e2 to either e3 or e4, but the d3 pawn has already left its initial position and has no choice; it can only move to d4.

Determine how the black pawns can move in this diagram.

There is a saying that every soldier carries a marshal's baton in his pack, but only he who has distinguished himself in battle gets a promotion. A brave pawn may not remain a pawn forever. If it reaches the last rank (the eighth rank for White or the first rank for Black), it is promoted, i.e. **changed into any piece of its colour, except for the king,** no matter whether any pieces of this kind remain on the board. Therefore, during a game, it is possible for several queens, rooks, bishops and knights to simultaneously participate, although it is unusual for more than two promotions to occur in a single game.

It is for the player to decide into which piece he will change his pawn. Most often the choice is the queen, the most powerful piece on the board. In such cases we say that a pawn is **promoted to a**

queen (alternatively **is queened,** or **queens**).

Now let's see what a pawn promotion looks like.

24

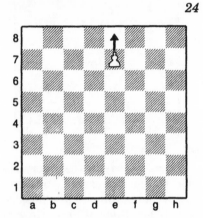

White moves his pawn to e8 and then removes the pawn from the board and puts any piece in its place. If it is a queen, then the move is written as e8♕.

The next diagram shows the position after the promotion of the pawn to a queen.

The square on which a pawn is exchanged for another piece is known as a **promotion** or **queening square**. In our example it was the e8-square.

When it moves to a promotion square, a pawn is forced to change into a piece as part of the same move. It at once acquires the rights of the new piece.

The pawn is the only participant of the chess battle which

25

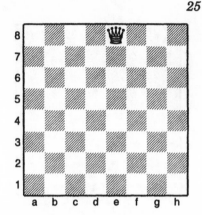

attacks the enemy in a different way to its normal (non-capturing) move. The pawn moves along a file but captures enemy men by making a forward diagonal move to an adjacent file.

26

The white pawn on d5 has no right to attack the bishop on d6

that is in its way but can capture the c6-knight or the e6-pawn that are diagonally forwards.

The black pawn on e6 can choose between the move e6-e5 and the capture of the white pawn on d5.

Owing to its ability to strike sideways, the pawn can attack two enemy pieces at the same time.

27

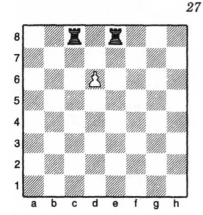

After d6-d7 both black rooks are attacked and one of them must perish. The double attack of a pawn is called a **pawn fork**.

It remains for us to learn one more cunning move of the pawn, the *en passant* **capture**.

If White plays his pawn from f2 to f3, Black can take it with his pawn. You already know that from its initial position a pawn can move forward two squares at a time, so what happens if White chooses the move f2-f4? The pawn tries to slip past the f3-square

28

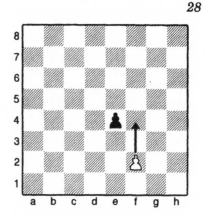

where it could be taken, but such a two-square dash does not remain unpunished. In this case Black is allowed to capture the cunning pawn exactly as if it had moved to the square f3.

29

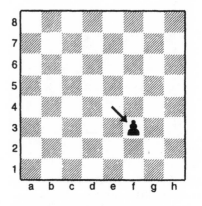

Here is the position after the *en passant* capture.

Note that only pawns can capture *en passant* and only after a two-square move of the enemy pawn. Moreover, the option to capture *en passant* must be exercised immediately; if you do not take the pawn immediately, then you cannot do so on the following move.

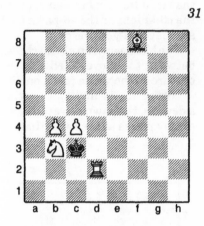

31

(6) Which pieces can the black king capture and which pieces are safe from capture? Why?

Exercises

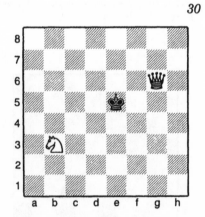

30

(5) To which squares can the black king move and to which squares can it not move? Why?

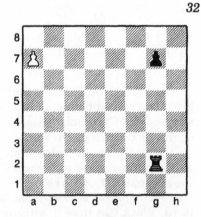

32

(7) White wants to play a7-a8 and promote his pawn to a queen. Can Black prevent it?

33

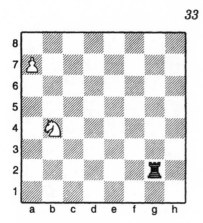

(8) And here?

35

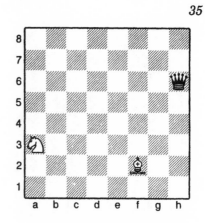

(10) How should the black queen move in order to attack the white bishop and white knight at the same time?

34

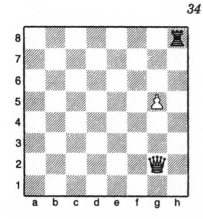

(9) How can you attack the black rook with the queen without exposing the latter to attack?

36

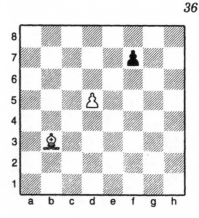

(11) How should White play in order to attack the black pawn on f7?

37

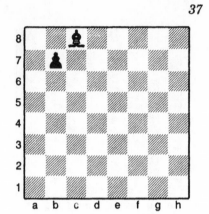

(12) In how many moves can the bishop get to the a6 square?

39

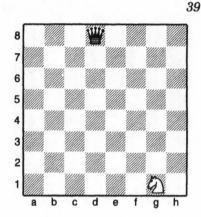

(14) In four consecutive moves the white knight must take Black's queen, without at any stage being exposed to the queen's attack.

38

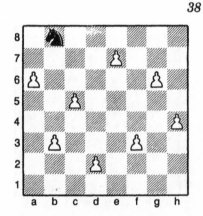

(13) In eight consecutive moves the black knight must capture all the white pawns.

40

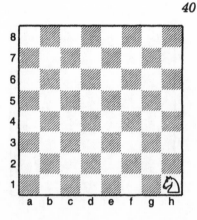

(15) Move the knight so that it visits every corner of the board just once and returns to h1 in 20 moves.

41

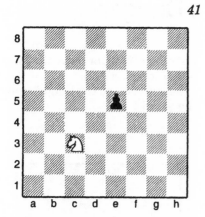

(16) How many moves does the white knight on c3 need to capture the e5-pawn?

42

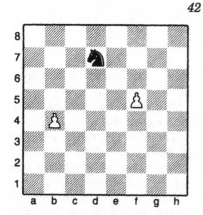

(17) What is the minimum number of moves required for the black knight on d7 to take both the white pawns?

43

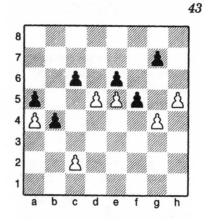

(18) Figure out all captures by the white and black pawns. How can Black reply to the move c2-c4 and White to the move g7-g5?

When the King is in Danger

What happens when the king is threatened by an enemy man? This means that the king is in check. It is warned: beware!

bishop on f8 (2), or move the king to the square h7 (3).

Let us remove the knight from the board.

44

45

The king is checked by the rook. It must not be left under attack; the assault must be repelled.

There are three ways of defending the king:

(1) to take the attacking piece,

(2) to shield the king being attacked with its own piece or pawn,

(3) to move the king to a vacant square that is not under enemy attack.

In this diagram we illustrate all three possibilities. Black can either capture the rook with his knight (1), or shield the king with the

Black has now two possibilities, ...♝f8 or ...♚h7.

Suppose we remove the bishop (see diagram 46).

The only possibility of escape is ...♚h7.

Now we move the pawn from h6 to h7 (see diagram 47).

There is no defence now. The squares f8 and h8 are also under the fire of the rook. The position is checkmate and White has won the game.

Therefore **a check is an attack against the opponent's king with a piece or a pawn**.

46

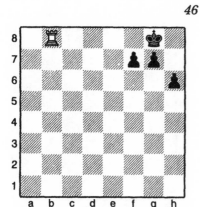

48

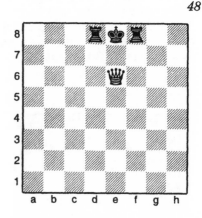

47

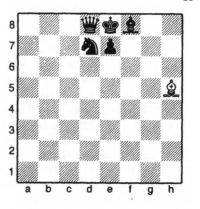

allow the king to move to the squares d7, e7 and f7. This type of mate is called an **epaulette mate** because the rooks on both sides of the king resemble the epaulettes on the shoulders of a general. They cut the king off from possible routes of escape.

49

A mate is a check against which there is no defence.

Under favourable conditions any piece can checkmate the enemy king. You have just seen how it can be done with the rook. We will see the other men perform the same task.

Here is a position where the queen mates; the queen does not

The bishop delivers mate. The black pieces are not only powerless to help their sovereign, they even prevent the king slipping away from the bishop's attack.

51

In this example the bishop has helped the queen.

50

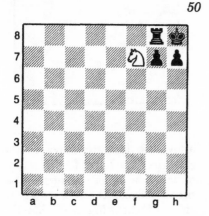

This is a peculiar mate. It is known as a **smothered mate**, because the king perishes as if being smothered by its own pieces. Here we can appreciate the knight's peculiar jumping ability.

However, it is not very often that a lone piece can finish off the enemy king single-handed. More often the mate is a result of joint efforts by two or more pieces.

The queen moves to e7 and checkmates. If there was no white bishop on b4, the king would simply take the queen off the board, but here the queen is defended by the bishop and according to the rules the king cannot move to a square covered by an enemy man.

52

Here the white bishop mates the king by moving to c6; the queen cuts off the escape routes on d8, e7, f7 or f8.

The knight could have also done the job:

53

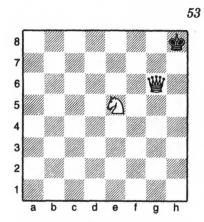

White plays ♘f7#.
In the next example the knight supports the queen.

54

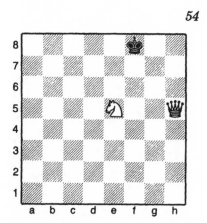

White can play ♕f7#.
In diagram 55 it supports the rook, so ♖h7# finishes Black.

The pawn supports the queen in diagram 56: ♕g7#.

55

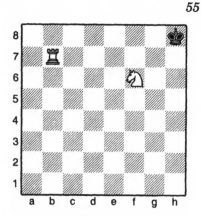

56

The number of mating positions is astronomical. It is impossible to memorise all of them, but during the game you must carefully watch the enemy king in order not to miss the moment for a decisive blow; of course, you must also ensure the safety of your own king.

Exercices

57

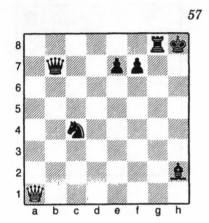

(19) White's queen has checked the black king. Indicate all the possibilities of defence.

59

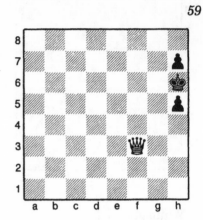

(21) White to play. Mate in one move.

58

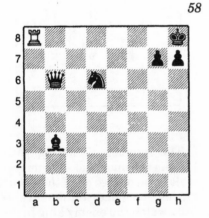

(20) Here the white rook has checked. Find the best defence.

60

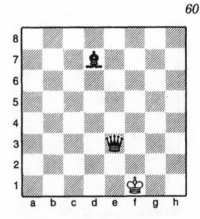

(22) Black to play. Mate in one move.

61

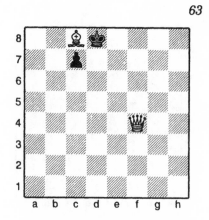

(23) White to play and mate in one move.

62

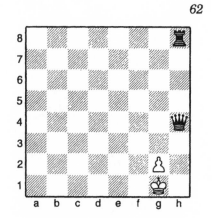

(24) Black to play and mate in one move.

63

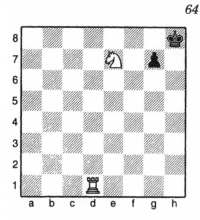

(25) White to play and mate in one move.

64

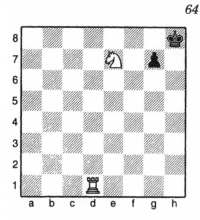

(26) White to play and mate in one move.

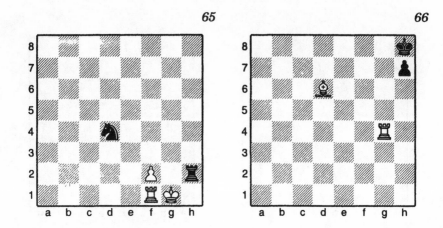

(27) Black to play and mate in one move.

(28) White to play and mate in one move.

Tied Hand and Foot

If a piece or a pawn blocks an enemy attack on the king it, like a sentry, cannot easily leave its post. Such a chessman loses much of its mobility and becomes static as if tied hand and foot. In chess we call it **a pinned piece**.

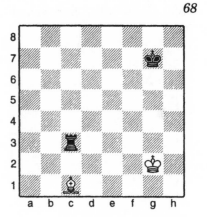

68

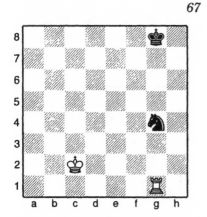

67

The knight is attacked by the rook, but if it leaves its post it will expose the king to attack, which is not allowed. There are no other pieces to defend the knight and so it is doomed. A pin often leads to the capture of an enemy piece.

Bishops move diagonally and can pin the enemy pieces in the direction of their movement.

In the following diagram White plays ♗b2 and the rook must perish.

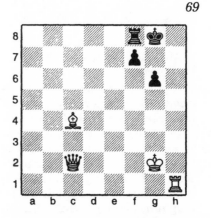

69

Here the f7-pawn seems to defend the g6-pawn, but this is not really true. It only protects the black king from the bishop on b3 and cannot do any other job. This

means that the g6 pawn is really
without defence, and therefore the
white queen can capture it and
checkmate the enemy king.

It is profitable to pin more valuable pieces with less valuable
ones.

71

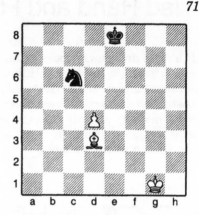

70

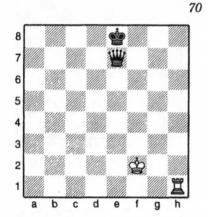

72

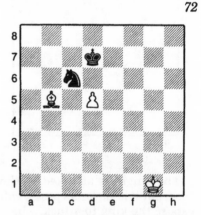

After ♖e1 White wins the queen
for the rook.

A pin leaves a chessman para-
lysed only temporarily and one
must make the most of this time.

In our next example (diagrams
71 and 72) the knight is ready to
take the d4-pawn but White plays
♗b5 and the knight is immobilised. Black can only defend the
knight by playing ...♔d7 with the
hope of breaking out of the pin
after the move ...♔d7-d6. For the
moment, though, the pin remains
in place. By playing d5, White attacks the knight a second time
and wins it.

However helpless a pinned piece
is, it always behaves aggressively
towards the enemy king.

In the diagram on the next
page the rook is pinned by the
bishop and cannot leave the d5-
square. Nevertheless, it cuts the
white king off from the e4-square
because it still controls the d-file.

73

74

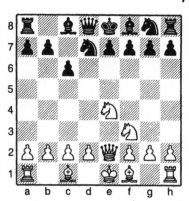

The king has no right to stand within the capturing range of even a pinned piece.

The pin is a crafty weapon and can easily be overlooked during the game. Diagrams 74 and 75 show the end of a game played at an international tournament.

Not suspecting a trap, Black played ...♘gf6 and all of a sudden White played ♘d6 mate! The knight is invulnerable since the white queen pins the e7-pawn along the e-file.

It remains to say that this catastrophe occurred as early as the sixth move of the game and that the Estonian Grandmaster Paul Keres was White and the Polish

75

Master G.Arlamovsky, who was not a novice at all, had the embarrassment of being Black.

Exercises

76

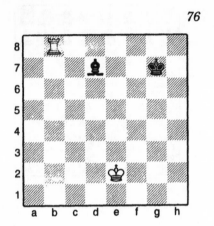

(29) Can White, to play, win the bishop?

77

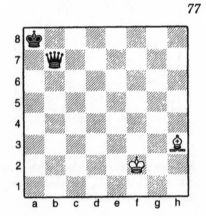

(30) Can White, to play, win the queen for the bishop?

78

(31) Can White, to play, win the knight?

79

(32) Can White, to play, win the rook without giving up the bishop?

80 81

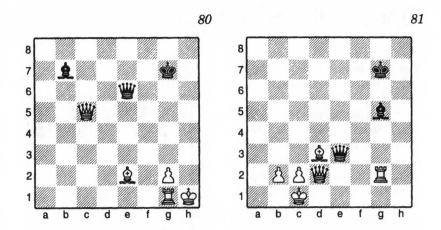

(33) Black to play. Mate in one move.

(34) Black is to move. What would you play?

Once in the King's Life

You have learned during the preceding lessons that the king is the main target for the enemy army and all your opponent's efforts are directed against it. At any moment the king may find itself in danger. However, the king has a special privilege based on a peculiar move differing from all other moves. This is **castling**, the only type of move in which two pieces, the king and a rook, are moved simultaneously. A player can castle only **once** during a game.

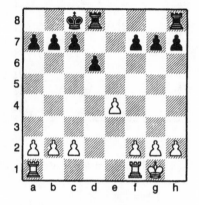

When castling, the king moves two squares in the direction of the rook and the rook jumps over it and lands in the square next to it. A player can castle on either side at his choice.

Here is the position after both sides have castled. White has castled on the kingside. This is called **short castling** and is written 0-0. Black has castled on the queenside. This is called **long castling** and is written as 0-0-0.

What is the difference between short and long castling? In kingside castling the rook moves two squares and in queenside castling it moves three squares. The resulting positions are also different. After kingside castling there is only one vacant square between the white king and the edge of the board whereas after queenside castling the black king has two vacant squares, a8 and b8. These distinctions may prove significant during a game. For instance, in diagram 83 the white pawn on h2 is protected by its king, whereas the black pawn on a7 is unprotected immediately after Black has castled.

Castling is not always possible. It is forbidden in the following cases.

(1) **Castling is forbidden if a piece, no matter whether one's own or the enemy's, occupies one of the squares between the king and the rook.**

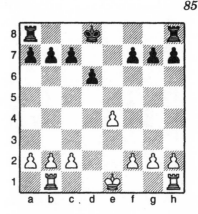

85

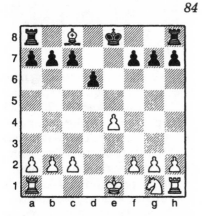

84

Here White can castle only on the queenside and Black only on the kingside.

(2) **Castling is forbidden if the king or the rook has already moved.**

The white rook that was initially on a1 has moved to b1, and therefore the white king cannot

castle on the queenside but can castle on the kingside, assuming that neither piece has moved earlier in the game. Note that even if White plays his rook from b1 back to a1, then he still cannot castle queenside. Once the rook on a1 moves, the possibility of white castling queenside is lost permanently.

The black king that was on e8 in its starting position has moved to d8. This means that Black has lost his right to castle. Even if the king returns to e8, then he cannot castle on either side of the board.

(3) **Castling is forbidden if the king is in check.**

The bishop has checked the king. White must either protect the king by advancing his pawn to c3 or he must move his king. The king cannot escape check by castling.

86

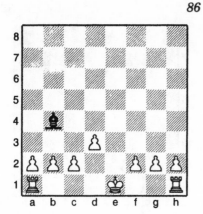

(4) Castling is forbidden if the king is in check after castling.

88

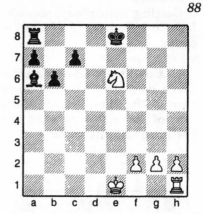

87

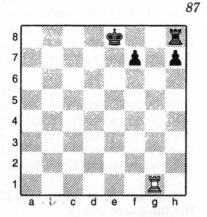

In the diagram immediately above, Black has no right to castle because on g8 his king would be exposed to the attack of the white rook.

When castling the white king must pass over the square f1; as this square is attacked by the black bishop on a6, castling is impossible. Black cannot castle either as his king must pass over d8, which is attacked by the white knight.

These rules often come into play during a game, because they can be used to prevent the enemy king from castling.

In diagram 89 Black would like to castle, but White moves the bishop to h6 and castling becomes impossible. In his turn, Black can prevent White from castling by moving his bishop to g4 (or a4).

The rules explained in the above two diagrams apply only to the king. The rook can cross an attacked square with impunity.

89

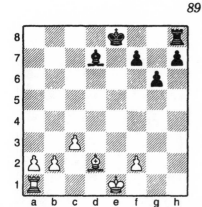

90

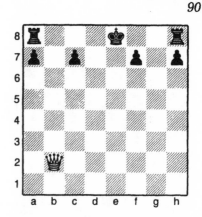

In diagram 90 the white queen on b2 controls the square b8 and attacks the rook on h8. However, this does not prevent Black from castling on either side.

Thus castling is a method of quickly evacuating the king to a safe shelter. It allows the king to abandon the centre of the board and to quickly hide in the corner behind a wall of pawns. If neither the king nor the rook has moved, a player can castle on any move when the possibility arises. It is usually done early on during the game since it is important to provide the king with a safe shelter before starting any aggressive action. Castling also makes it possible for the rook to enter the battle at an early stage. For instance, in queenside castling the rook leaves the corner where it stood inactive and moves to an active position on the central d-file. The famous wit, Grandmaster Saviely Tartakower, called castling "the first step to a healthy life".

Exercises

91

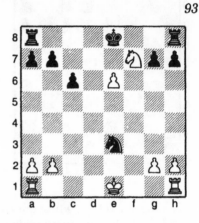

(35) Assuming that any kings and rooks standing on their original squares have never moved, on which sides can Black and White castle?

92

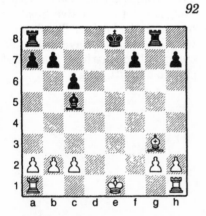

(36) And here?

93

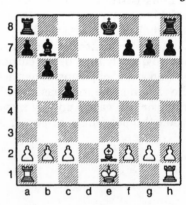

(37) And here?

94

(38) What should White play to prevent the enemy king from castling queenside? And what should Black play to prevent the white king from castling kingside?

Stalemate and Perpetual Check

A game of chess can result in **a win, a draw** or **a loss**. In normal tournament play a win earns one point, a draw half a point, and a loss ... nothing.

Not every game ends with mate. Sometimes one of the players resigns before mate is actually delivered, admitting the fact that his position is hopeless. But how can a chess game be drawn?

You have perhaps heard of "grandmaster draws". This term ironically refers to short games in which for some reason or other the players do not want to continue the game and agree to a draw when the board is full of pieces. In such cases people say that the opponents parted in peace having no time to quarrel.

The refusal to fight and an excessive tendency to agree early draws contradicts the point of playing chess. Almost all eminent chess players rarely agree "grandmaster draws". World Champion Garry Kasparov and Grandmasters Nigel Short, Jan Timman, Viswanathan Anand, Artur Yusupov and many others are notable for their uncompromising style. They usually agree to a draw only when all possibilities of further play are exhausted. Young chess players must learn to fight without thinking of the result, and not fear attacking even strong opponents. The result may be a loss today, but the experience gained from these games will mean wins in the future.

However, chess is unthinkable without the possibility of a draw. There are many positions in which a draw is unavoidable, for example when only the kings remain on the board. In the subsequent chapters you will become familiar with some other drawn positions. Here we shall study two very important situations that lead to a draw.

95

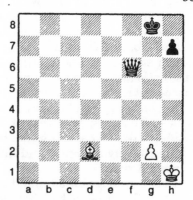

White is to play and the correct continuation is ♗c3, which allows the player to give mate with the queen on g7 after Black moves his

pawn. Does playing the bishop to
h6 amount to the same thing?

96

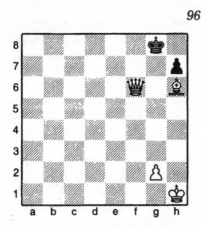

An interesting situation has occurred. It is Black's turn to play
but he has no legal move. The
king is not allowed to move into
check and the h7 pawn is blocked
by the white bishop. Is it a checkmate? No, as Black's king is not
under attack. It is **stalemate**, i.e.
a situation when the king is not in
check but neither the king nor its
army have any legal moves. The
rules of chess specify that **if a
stalemate arises, the game is
immediately stopped and de-
clared drawn**.

Between diagram 95 and diagram 96 the situation has changed
in Black's favour, since White has
large material preponderance in
diagram 95.

Suppose that in diagram 96 we
move the black queen to a8.

97

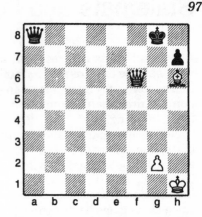

There is no stalemate for Black
here because his queen has legal
moves. How can Black prevent
the mate on g7? If he plays ...♛a7
or ...♛b7, the white queen will
give mate on the square f8 instead. Black is losing only because
of his queen. As we have seen, if it
were not for the queen, Black
would be in stalemate. Can Black
get rid of his queen somehow?
Not by putting it in his pocket
while the opponent is distracted,
but by sacrificing it in such a way
that the stalemate position is pre-
served.

If Black exposes his queen, say,
by playing ...♛c6 or ...♛f3, White
will ignore it and give mate on g7.
Hence Black must sacrifice his
queen in such a way that White
will have to take it, for example
by making the move ...♛a1+.
White must take the black queen
with his own (otherwise, when

the white king moves, Black will capture the white queen on f6). However, the black king would then have the square f7 at its disposal and the stalemate would have disappeared.

The only solution is for the black queen to sacrifice itself by capturing the g2-pawn. The white king is in check. It must take the queen since it is the only defence to the check.

98

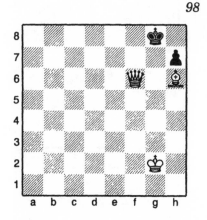

The resulting position is similar to position 96. Black is to play, but he has no legal moves and so he is in stalemate and the game is drawn. Black has averted defeat.

Be careful and fight to the very end. Remember that stalemate is the last hope of a king that is in distress.

Here is one more device that can be used to reduce a game to a draw.

Have you ever attempted to invent "perpetual motion"? Science proved this to be impossible, but chess players invented, if not "perpetual motion", then something like it, namely **perpetual check**.

99

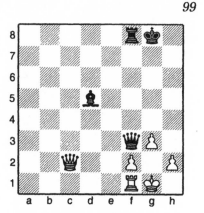

The white king is in mortal danger as it is threatened with mate on g2 or h1. There is no direct defence, but it is White's turn to play and he is the first to attack the enemy king: ♕g6+. The king must move, ...♔h8. The queen keeps pursuing by ♕h6+. The king must again side-step in order to get out of check, ...♔g8. The queen keeps chasing it and everything is repeated, ♕g6+, and so on until you grow a beard.

This is a **perpetual check**. It means a situation when **one of the players endlessly checks the opponent's king but can't** checkmate it. Neither side can win and **the game is considered to end in a draw**. Perpetual check can sometimes save you when you are in an apparently hopeless situation.

Exercises

100

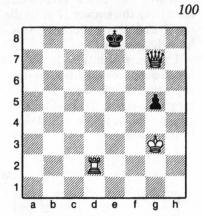

(39) Black to play. Is it stalemate or not?

101

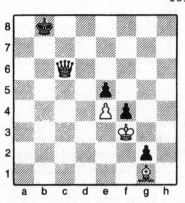

(40) And here?

102

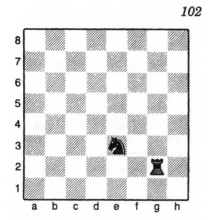

(41) Which square must the white king occupy to be in stalemate? (Two solutions.)

104

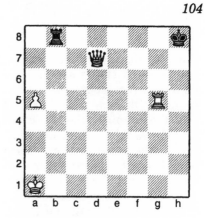

(43) Black to play. Can he avert defeat?

103

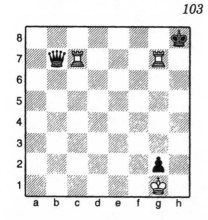

(42) White to play. Can he win the queen?

105

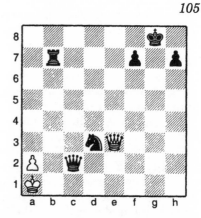

(44) White to play. Can he avert defeat?

Without a Hitch

For a layman, chess language is double-dutch. Have you ever heard chess players speaking after a match? "Oh", one might say, "if I took the f3-knight, then the check on g5 would be unavoidable". "But," the other objects, "then I would pin the queen on e7 with the rook on b2." And the passers-by wonder: "What gibberish!"

Once, in 1891, Mikhail Chigorin and the World Champion Wilhelm Steinitz, who lived in America, played a match of two games. Moves were wired. The unusual text of the telegrams made the New York police suspicious and one day Steinitz was arrested as a Russian spy and was accused of wiring secret information by means of a special code!

This "code", i.e. the system of writing down the squares and moves, is called chess notation. When you master it, you will be able to read chess books and periodicals where you will find descriptions of games played by masters and grandmasters. By playing over these games on your board and studying the methods and techniques of top players, you will supplement your knowledge and perfect your skill.

You have already learnt some parts of chess notation while studying the preceding chapters. The following table includes the main symbols:

x = capture
0-0 = kingside castling
0-0-0 = queenside castling
+ = check
 # = checkmate (sometimes the word itself is written instead of the symbol)

Let us now learn how to record a game from the very beginning to the end. There are two kinds of chess notation, **full** and **abbreviated**.

When using full notation, you first record the square on which a chess piece stands before the move. This is the square of departure. The square to which you move the piece is the point of arrival. The moves are numbered; after a pair of moves, one white and one black, there is a "move number". This helps when referring to the game later on, e.g.: "On move 23, White should have moved his queen to g4." Thus you put down the number of a move, then the move made by White and the move made by Black.

Set up the chessmen in the starting position and play the following short game.

**1 e2-e4 e7-e5 2 Ng1-f3 Nb8-c6
3 Bf1-b5 a7-a6 4 Bb5-a4 Bf8-c5**

5 0-0 Ng8-f6 6 c2-c3 Bc5-a7 7 Rf1-e1 Nf6-g4 8 d2-d4 e5xd4 9 c3xd4 Nc6xd4 10 Nf3xd4 Qd8-h4 11 Nd4-f3 Qh4xf2+ 12 Kg1-h1 Qf2-g1+ 13 Nf3xg1 Ng4-f2#.

106

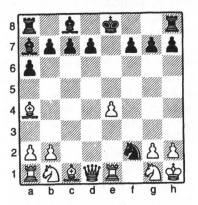

This is the final position of the above game. When writing down a position, the pieces are arranged by seniority, and when the men are equal "in rank", you begin the record from the queenside. You first record the position of the white men and then that of the black men. The total number of pieces is sometimes written in brackets. For example, the position in the diagram above is written:

White: Kh1, Qd1, Ra1, Re1, Ba4, Bc1, Nb1, Ng1, Pa2, b2, e4, g2, h2 (13).

Black: Ke8, Ra8, Rh8, Ba7, Bc8, Nf2, Pa6, b7, c7, d7, f7, g7, h7 (13).

In the abbreviated notation only the square where a piece lands is recorded. Here is how the same game looks like in the abbreviated notation:

1 e4 e5 2 Nf3 Nc6 3 Bb5 a6 4 Ba4 Bc5 5 0-0 Nf6 6 c3 Ba7 7 Re1 Ng4 8 d4 ed 9 cd Nd4 10 Nd4 Qh4 11 Nf3 Qxf2+ 12 Kh1 Qg1+ 13 Nxg1 Nf2#.

You already know that in different languages the names of chessmen are different, and therefore, to make chess notation international, the names of the pieces (but not pawns) are often replaced by their graphic representations. We use them in this book. Here is the record of the same game in which the men are shown by symbols.

1 e4 e5 2 ♘f3 ♘c6 3 ♗b5 a6 4 ♗a4 ♗c5 5 0-0 ♘f6, etc.

The abbreviated notation has some peculiarities. Here are two examples illustrating them.

Look at the diagram on the next page. Suppose that White decides to move the rook from h1 to e1. In the full notation this move is clear: ♖h1-e1. Now if you abbreviate the notation, i.e. write ♖e1, an ambiguity arises. It is not clear which of the rooks landed on the e1 square since both rooks could have done this. Therefore one more letter, to make the square of departure clear, must be added, ♖he1 in this case. Clearly, the move with the rook from c1 to e1 is written as ♖ce1.

107

The same method applies to the knights. For instance, either black knight can occupy the square f6. If it is the g8-knight, then we must write ...♘gf6 and if the d7-knight, then ...♘df6.

108

Here, too, we deal with rooks and knights, but here the two similar pieces stand on one file. In such cases the square of departure is denoted by the number of the corresponding rank.

For instance, you can move the rook from c1 to c4 and write ♖1c4, which means that the rook which was on the first rank moved to c4. Moving the rook from c7 to c4 is written as ♖7c4.

Both black knights can move to either d5 or h5. If the move is made by the f6-knight, then you write ...♘6d5 or ...♘6h5 and if it is made by the f4 knight, then you write ...♘4d5 or ...♘4h5.

The explanations took more time than the move itself; in fact all this is very simple and when you gain experience, you will record your games automatically, without much thinking.

In chess literature you will find games followed by explanations (often called notes or comments). Masters and grandmasters explain the reasons behind the moves played and what would happen if they played differently. It is customary to evaluate moves according to certain symbols. Here are some of them.

! = a good move
!! = an excellent move
? = a poor move, a mistake
?? = a very bad move, a blunder
!? = a move deserving attention
?! a risky (dubious) move

You may encounter many more symbols in special theoretical literature. You will get acquainted with them when you become more experienced.

Exercises

(45) Play over this game: 1 e4 c6 2 ♘c3 d5 3 d4 de 4 ♘xe4 ♘f6 5 ♘xf6+ exf6 6 ♗c4 ♗e7 7 ♕h5 0-0 8 ♘e2 g6 9 ♕f3 ♘d7 10 ♗h6 ♖e8 11 ♗xf7+ ♔xf7 12 ♕b3 mate.

(46) Write down this game in full notation.

(47) Record the final position of the chessmen.

(48) Set up the men in the following position.

White: ♘d1, ♘d3, ♙c7. Black: ♖a7, ♖g7, ♙f2.

White can capture the f2-pawn with either of the knights. In his turn, Black can capture the c7-pawn with either of his rooks. Write down all the possible captures for both sides using abbreviated notation.

(49) Set up the following position on the board. White: ♖b1, ♖b8, ♙f3. Black: ♘e5, ♘h4, ♙b5. Write down all possible captures by White and Black using abbreviated notation.

The Lone King

The king that has lost its army has a poor lot. It has no place to hide; enemies are all around. Whatever direction it takes, it is in danger. Nevertheless, the king does not lose hope. The rules of chess leave it a chance, in that if a lone king is not mated in 50 moves, and no pawn move or capture takes place in this time, the game is considered to be drawn. Moreover, the king always hopes for stalemate which also means a draw.

If you have the superior side, then to avoid such an embarrassment you should not aimlessly chase the enemy king up and down the board by checking it. Instead, you should think out a plan of action and not make useless moves.

The Last Line of Defence

It is easy to **mate with two rooks**. Here is one of the finishing positions which a player must strive to achieve.

As you can see, the rooks successfully cope with the enemy king unassisted. The execution takes place on the edge of the board, where the mobility of the enemy king is restricted. It stands to reason that all four sides of the board can serve this purpose equally well.

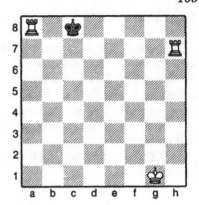

But how can you force the king to retreat to the back rank?

By means of successive checks the king is **driven** across the files and ranks and the rooks take turns in **cutting it off** from possible escape.

In diagram 110, you must first decide where you will drive the king. Suppose you have chosen the 8th rank. Now you can fulfil your plan.

1 ♖h3 (controlling the third rank, so cutting off the king's retreat) **1...♔e4 2 ♖g4+** (the other rook becomes a hunter forcing the king to retreat) **2...♔f5** (the retreating king attacks the rook, which must switch to the other side along the same rank; such a manoeuvre is known as a transfer)

110

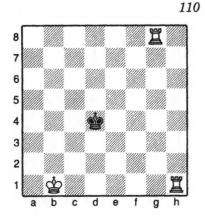

3 ♖a4 ♚e5 4 ♖h5+ (the rooks have changed roles and now the a4-rook becomes a guard and the h5-rook a hunter; this repeats until the king is driven to the 8th rank) **4...♚d6 5 ♖a6+ ♚c7 6 ♖h7+ ♚b8.**

111

8 7 6 5 4 3 2 1
a b c d e f g h

White has achieved his goal, the king has been forced to the edge of the board and has nowhere to retreat. Now White can **checkmate in two moves,** and he even has a choice of two tactical devices.

The first device is the transfer, which you already know. Since the a8-square is inaccessible to the a6-rook, it is transferred to the other side of the board, say, to g6 and checkmates (♖g8#) with the next move.

The other device is passing the move to Black. White reasons as follows: if in the diagram Black had to move, he would be forced to move his king to c8 (there is no other square). The king would no longer guard the square a8 and so the a6-rook would be able to checkmate.

Hence White must pass his move to Black while retaining all the advantages of the position. This can be attained by means of a **waiting move** which does not essentially change the position. White can make many moves of this kind, for example any move with the king, or with one of the rooks, for instance, ♖a5, ♖a4, etc., or ♖e7, ♖f7, ♖g7.

Black cannot simply wait and must move his king to c8 allowing the a6-rook to checkmate (♖a8#). A situation when it is not advantageous for a player to make a move but it is his turn to play is called **zugzwang.** Zugzwang is one of the most significant tactical devices in the endgame.

There is one more way of forcing the king to an edge of the board.

112

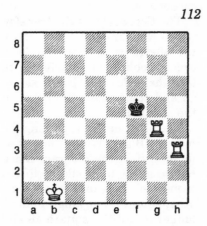

We already had this position in diagram 110 (after Black's second move). Here we suggested the move ♖g4-a4, i.e. a transfer of the rook; but we can win by a different method: **1 ♖hh4** (the rooks stand side by side and defend each other as if fighting hand in hand – see diagram 113)

1...♔e5 (to the move 1...♔f6 White replies 2 ♖h5, repeating the initial situation but with Black's king having been forced back by a rank) **2 ♖h5+ ♔f6 3 ♖gg5** (the rooks again "hold hands", a manoeuvre which is repeated until the end of the game) **3...♔e6 4 ♖h6+ ♔f7 5 ♖gg6 ♔e7 6 ♖h7+ ♔f8 7 ♖gg7 ♔e8** and either rook can checkmate along the 8th rank.

113

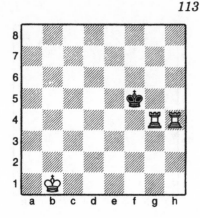

The Deadly Corridor

It is even easier to mate **with the queen and a rook** as the enemy king cannot approach the queen and, moreover, the queen protects the rook not only along the file and rank but also along the diagonal.

Here are some typical checkmate positions.

114

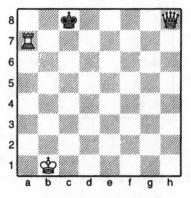

Diagram 114 is the same type of checkmate as with two rooks. If the rook and the queen change places, the picture remains the same.

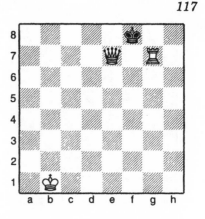

117

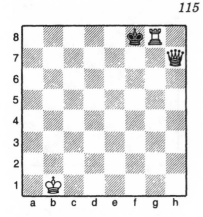

115

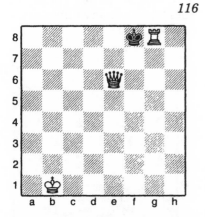

116

In diagrams 115 and 116 the mate is accomplished with the rook protected by the queen.

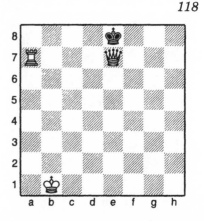

118

In the last three examples the queen checkmates aided by the rook's defence. It is even easier to force the enemy king to an edge of the board with a queen and a rook than with two rooks. In diagrams 117 and 118 the queen mates the king on the edge; in diagram 119 the king is mated in the corner.

119

120

play the role of "guard" and "hunter") **3...♔b6 4 ♕b8+ ♔a6 5 ♖a7 mate**.

121

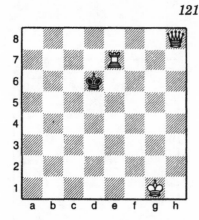

We encountered this position in diagram 120 after the moves 1 ♖e7 ♔d6. We played 2 ♕d8+ but could have won in a different way: **1 ♕e5+ ♔c6**

122

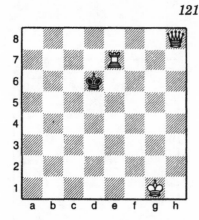

We can drive the black king to the a-file: **1 ♖e7** (the rook cuts the king off from the e-file) **1...♔d6** (the king attacks the rook but the queen comes to rescue) **2 ♕d8+** (the queen checks and at the same time protects the rook) **2...♔c6 3 ♖c7+** (as in the previous examples, White's pieces alternately

The black king is forced into a narrow passage on the 6th rank. At the end of this passage it will meet its death: **2 ♖c7+** (first the rook is defended by the queen) **2...♔b6 3 ♕c5+** (then the queen is defended by the rook) **3...♔a6 4 ♖a7 mate**.

While chasing the enemy king with the queen and the rook, you must avoid stalemate positions.

123

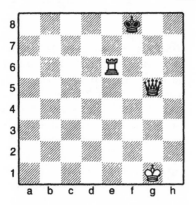

If White carelessly plays ♕g6 or ♖e7, then the black king will not have a single free square, and this, as you know, is stalemate, a drawn game. Hence do not hurry, let the king take his last breath of fresh air: **1 ♖e5 ♔f7** (now attack the enemy king) **2 ♖e7+ ♔f8 3 ♕g7 mate**. Other methods are also possible, for example **1 ♕g4 ♔f7 2 ♕g6+ ♔f8 3 ♖e8 mate** or **1 ♕f5+ ♔g7 2 ♖g6+ ♔h7 3 ♕h5 mate**.

A Strong Grip

It is difficult for one rook to cope with the king. At best the rook can threaten it with checks, and from a considerable distance at that. The problem can only be solved when the rook co-operates with its own king.

Here are two concluding positions which you must strive for when you play with a rook.

124

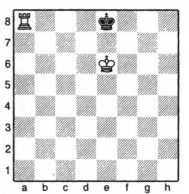

In diagram 124, the co-operation of the rook and the king makes it possible to force the enemy king to the edge of the board and finish it off.

However, it is impossible to force a mate on the edge of the board from a normal starting position. Instead, a corner mate, as in diagram 125, is the standard conclusion to a struggle of king and rook against king.

125

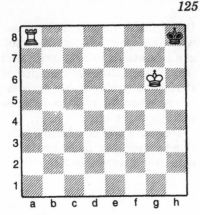

127

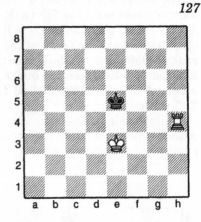

126

1 **♖h4** (occupying the 4th rank, the rook immediately cuts the black king off from half the board) **1...♚e5** (now White must move his king nearer) **2 ♚e2 ♚d5 3 ♚e3 ♚e5** (diagram 127)

The king does not want to retreat voluntarily, but here we have a position deserving special

attention. As soon as the kings face each other a square apart, the rook gets an opportunity to check the enemy king and force it one rank back. Such a confrontation of the kings is known as the **opposition**. You will frequently meet it: **4 ♖h5+** (it is easy to see that the rook plays here the part of a "hunter" and the white king that of a "guard"; Black must retreat) **4...♚d6** (diagram 128)

Which move must White make in order to attain the same relative position of the kings as shown in the previous diagram? You will say 5 ♚d4 and ... be mistaken. Black will play 5...♚e6 and to 6 ♚e4 reply with 6...♚d6, and White will only lose time.

White must be a little more clever. The kings need to be in opposition while it is White's turn to play and not Black's. Thus White should play **5 ♚e4!** (diagram 129)

128

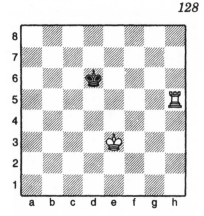

129

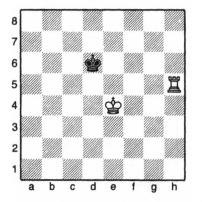

It is a good move. Now the white king is at the distance of a knight's move from Black's king as if inviting it to take the opposition, i.e. to occupy the square e6, a move which will be followed by a check with the rook from h6. It stands to reason that Black tries to avoid this: **5...♚c6 6 ♔d4** (the

white king again chases the enemy with the "knight's move") **6...♚b6 7 ♔c4 ♚a6 8 ♔b4 ♚b6** (the edge of the board has been reached and Black is forced to go back, but this is precisely what White wanted, namely, the opposition with him to move) **9 ♖h6+ ♚c7 10 ♔b5** (the situation repeats itself one rank higher) **10...♚d7 11 ♔c5 ♚e7 12 ♔d5 ♚f7 13 ♔e5 ♚g7** (the king attacks the rook, so White must take care) **14 ♖a6** (remember the device called a transfer) **14...♚f7 15 ♖b6** (this is a waiting move) **15...♚g7 16 ♔f5 ♚h7 17 ♔g5 ♚g7 18 ♖b7+ ♚f8** (like a hockey-player who has lingered, the king is forced to the touch-line; in the final phase, the checkmate involves a repetition of the earlier manoeuvres) **19 ♔g6 ♚e8 20 ♔f6 ♚d8 21 ♔e6 ♚c8 22 ♖h7 ♚d8 23 ♖g7 ♚c8 24 ♔d6 ♚b8 25 ♔c6 ♚a8 26 ♔b6 ♚b8 27 ♖g8 mate**.

Here is a more efficient and, therefore, quicker way of checkmating (see diagram 130).

We have had this position, it arose in the previous diagram after Black's move 7...♚a6. Then we continued 8 ♔b4, but we could have achieved our object much faster: **1 ♖b5!** (the enemy king is cut off along the b-file from the rest of the board) **1...♚a7 2 ♔c5 ♚a6 3 ♖b1** (as in the preceding example, the king is now at the knight's move from the black king and waits for the latter to

130

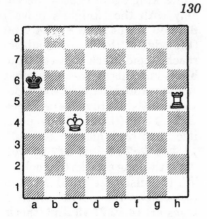

take the opposition) **3...♔a7 4 ♔c6 ♔a8 5 ♔c7 ♔a7 6 ♖a1 mate**, now along the a-file.

The Chase

The queen has the powers of a rook, so it can imitate the rook and create the mating positions you already know, such as this one.

131

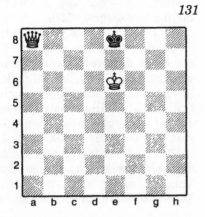

The ability to move like a bishop allows the queen to create considerably more mating positions:

132

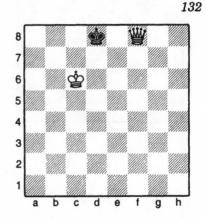

133

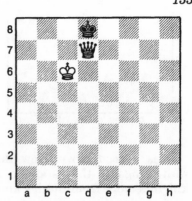

In diagrams 132-134 the queen attacks the enemy king and prevents its escape not only along a file and a rank (like a rook) but

134

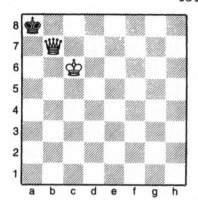

135

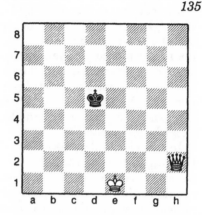

also along a diagonal (like a bishop).

Thanks to its many powers, the queen can force the enemy king to the side of the board all by itself. However, to give checkmate, even the queen requires help from its king. In certain cases the king prevents the enemy king's escape (diagrams 131 and 132) and in other cases (diagrams 133 and 134) it protects the queen.

The queen is unrivalled in creating mating positions, because its powers exceed that of any other piece.

Let us consider a manoeuvre called a "chase", where, up to a certain point, the queen acts alone.

The first problem is to force the black king to an edge of the board without the aid of the king.

1 ♕f4 (note that the queen stands at a knight's move from the black king; in this position it considerably restricts the king's mobility, making it gradually retreat to the edge of the board) **1...♚c5 2 ♕e4 ♚d6** (White replies to 2...♚b5 with **3 ♕d4** and to 2...♚b6 with **3 ♕d5**) **3 ♕f5 ♚c6 4 ♕e5** (the same idea again) **4...♚b6 5 ♕d5 ♚c7 6 ♕e6 ♚b7 7 ♕d6 ♚c8 8 ♕e7 ♚b8 9 ♕d7 ♚a8**

136

Now is the time to take care; if White continues the chase by 10 ♕c7??, then stalemate will occur and the game will be drawn. It is not a very pleasant experience to draw with an extra queen. These are the situations a careless player may find himself in even when the positions are very simple. Don't be too hasty!

In diagram 136 we have forced the king to the last rank, i.e. successfully coped with the first problem. Now we should leave it at least one possible move and proceed to solve the second problem, that of bringing the king up to help. Remember that the pieces must assist one another: **10 ♔d2 ♔b8 11 ♔c3 ♔a8 12 ♔b4 ♔b8 13 ♔b5 ♔a8** (the black king rushes about like a mouse in a trap but cannot escape its fate) **14 ♔b6 ♔b8**, and the queen gives mate from one of three squares at your choice, b7 d8 or e8.

It is possible to checkmate with the king and queen more quickly if these pieces combine their efforts as shown in the next example.

1 ♕e4+ ♔d6 2 ♔c4 ♔d7 3 ♔c5 ♔c7 4 ♕c6+ ♔b8 (see diagram 138)

It would be easy to make a mistake here. After the careless 5 ♔b6?? the black king would be stalemated.

The right method is **5 ♕d7 ♔a8 6 ♔b6 ♔b8**, and the queen checkmates.

137

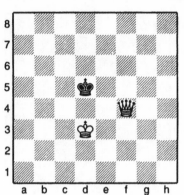

138

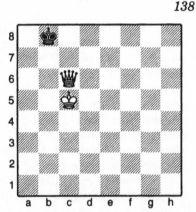

Close Friends

A lone bishop cannot win against a lone king even if it is assisted by its king. At best the bishop can check but never checkmate.

However much White tries, the black king always finds a vacant square. The most that White can

139

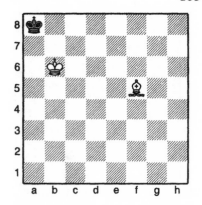

together they can finish off the lone king.

attain is a stalemate, e.g. after the moves **1 ♗e4+ ♚b8 2 ♗b7**. Or, with a dark-squared bishop:

140

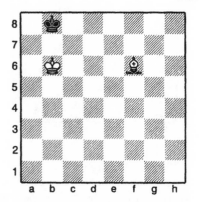

1 ♗e5+ ♚a8 2 ♚a6 stalemate. It is useless to continue with a king and bishop against a king; the game is drawn. However, if White has one more bishop, then

141

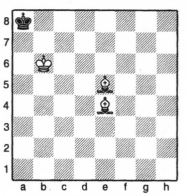

If the corner square is a light colour, then the light-squared bishop strikes the final blow and the other bishop joins the king in cutting the enemy off from every possibility of escape.

142

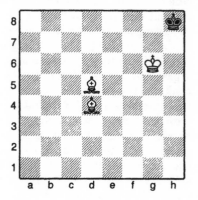

If the corner square is dark, then the dark-squared bishop becomes a "hunter".

In order to cut off the enemy king from a part of the board, the bishops must act on adjacent diagonals.

144

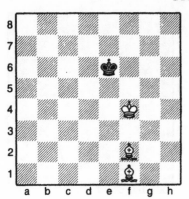

143

In this position the bishops create an impassable barrier cutting the enemy king off from the other side of the board. White can win by maintaining the barrier and executing an outflanking manoeuvre with his king. Black's king is caught in a pincer movement and is gradually driven, first to the 8th rank and then to the corner square h8: 1 ♔g2 ♚e4 2 ♔g3 ♚d5 3 ♔f4 ♚e6 (diagram 144) 4 ♗g2 (the barrier has moved to the next diagonal and the bishops keep all the loopholes closed) 4...♚d6 5 ♔f5 ♚e7 6 ♗g3 ♚d7 7 ♔f6 ♚d8 8 ♗h3 ♚e8 (diagram 145).

145

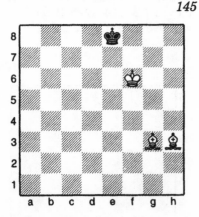

The black king is forced to the edge of the board. It must now be driven into the corner, to the square h8: 9 ♗c7 (White's dark-squared bishop cuts off the black king from the escape route via d8) 9...♚f8 10 ♗d7 (now the light-squared bishop takes over the job) 10...♚g8 11 ♔g6 (the king stops the enemy from slipping away to h7) **11...♚f8**

146

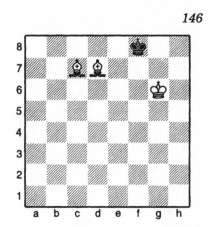

The finish runs: **12 ♗d6+ ♚g8 13 ♗e6+ ♚h8 14 ♗e5 mate**.

Note that, as in all the preceding examples, the white king tried all the time to occupy a square a knight's move away from the black king.

147

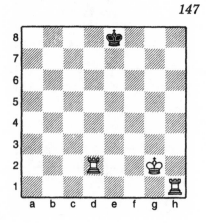

(50) White to play. Mate in two moves.

148

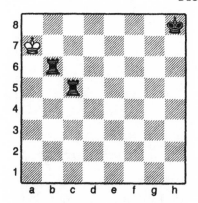

(51) Black to play. Mate in two moves.

149

151

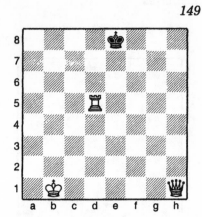

(52) White to play. Mate in two moves.

(54) White to play. Mate in two moves (three solutions).

150

152

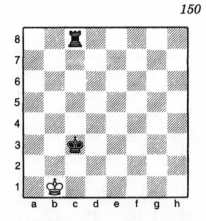

(53) Black to play. Mate in two moves (two solutions).

(55) White to play. Mate in three moves (two solutions).

To Take or Not to Take?

You have just seen how different pieces can checkmate a lone king. The queen could do this quicker and more easily than the rook and the rook could mate more easily than two bishops. However, forcing mate is beyond the power of a lone bishop or a lone knight. This means that chessmen are not equal in strength, some of them are stronger and others are weaker. How is their strength measured? Just as the cost of goods is valued in dollars, marks, roubles and pounds, lifting capacity is measured in tons and speed in miles per hour, so **the value of chessmen** has its unit of measurement. A pawn, the most humble participant of a chess game, serves as this unit.

Here is the price-list of chess values:

Bishop = 3
Knight = 3
Rook = 5
Queen = 9
Pawn = 1

The king has no value since it cannot be "sold". When the king perishes, the game ends.

The strongest piece is the queen and the next strongest is the rook. They are called **major pieces**. The bishop and the knight are less valuable, they are **minor pieces**. If you give up a rook for a bishop or a knight, you lose **the exchange** since the rook costs two points more.

What does the **relative value of the chessmen depend on?** It depends on the number of squares each of them controls, i.e. on their mobility and range. It is quite clear from the table on the next page.

The men that control a greater number of squares affect the game more and therefore their value is higher. There is an odd coincidence in this in that the value of the knight and the bishop is the same. Although the bishop is a long-range piece, it controls only squares of one colour, i.e. only half the board, either 32 light squares or 32 dark squares. The knight can gallop over all 64 squares and can jump over other men, but can only act at short range. It turns out that the pros and cons balance each other, so that the bishop and knight are of roughly equal value.

You must always remember the relative values of the pieces so that you do not give up a more valuable piece for a less valuable one. If this happens, then you are the loser and your opponent gains a **material advantage**. The larger

Chessmen	The number of squares a man controls on an empty board		Value of the men in pawns
	at the center	in a corner	
Queen	27	21	9
Rook	14	14	5
Bishop	13	7	3
Knight	8	2	3
Pawn	2	1	1

this advantage, the easier it is to gain victory.

Once, playing against his main rival Johann Zukertort, Wilhelm Steinitz found himself in a hopeless position and on the point of being mated but he did not want to resign and continued his hopeless resistance. Suddenly Zukertort ceased attacking the enemy king and began moving his pawns on the other side of the board.

"Why do you move your pawns?" asked Steinitz in surprise.

"I'll queen two pawns and then occupy myself with your king," Zukertort quietly answered.

The threat had an effect and Steinitz immediately resigned.

You already know that attack and defence are the main tactical devices in a chess game. During a game the pieces constantly interact and the problem often arises as to whether a player should take an enemy piece in exchange for one of his own. To take or not to

take? In most cases you should decide on the basis of the table of values given above.

Let us analyse the beginning of a game.

1 e4 e5 2 ♘f3

White attacks the e5-pawn with a knight.

2...♘c6

Black defends it. After 3 ♘xe5 follows 3...♘xe5. To whose advantage is this operation? To Black's, of course. He would take the knight at a low price, for only one pawn, because the knight is three times as valuable.

3 ♗b5 a6

The pawn attacks the bishop. White has to decide whether he should take the knight with the bishop or not. As you know, the bishop and the knight are of the same value, and therefore he will not get any material advantage.

4 ♗xc6 dc

As a result of an exchange two equivalent pieces were removed from the board. The balance of material remains intact. Now, however, the e5-pawn is defenceless. White tries to make use of this.

5 ♘xe5

White has won a pawn and thereby gained a material advantage. Is it for long?

5...♕d4

The queen attacks the knight on e5 and the e4-pawn at the same time. The two pieces cannot be defended by one move. Which piece should be saved? The knight, of course, because it is more valuable.

6 ♘f3 ♕xe4+

Black has won back his pawn and thus restored material equality.

7 ♕e2 ♕xe2+ 8 ♔xe2

An exchange of queens has occurred. White and Black are again equal in strength and can quietly continue the game.

Material advantage is not always the decisive factor in the choice of a move. Sometimes a player intentionally runs the risk of a material loss to gain other advantages, for example the ability to attack the king. This is known as a **sacrifice**. Sacrifices introduce surprises into the game and make it more interesting.

One Moscow chess player of the last century once confessed that he was afraid of playing against Mikhail Chigorin.

"Why?" he was asked.

"I am always afraid that he will sacrifice a piece..."

Set up the pieces in the starting position and play the following short game:

1 e4 e5 2 ♘f3 d6 3 ♗c4 g6

A bad move which beginners are often inclined to make. You must not lose time at the beginning of a game, the main thing is to develop inactive pieces. 3...♗e7 would be a better move.

4 ♘c3 ♗g4?

This is a terrible mistake. However, it is not so easy to find the refutation.

153

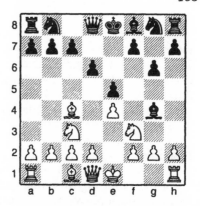

5 ♘xe5! ♗xd1??

5...dxe5 would be the lesser evil, reconciling himself to the loss of a pawn after 6 ♕xg4. The move in the game looks more tempting, because Black has won the most powerful piece, the queen! Perhaps White simply overlooked it?

No, he sacrificed it having in mind an effective finish.

6 ♗xf7+ ♚e7 7 ♘d5 mate!

154

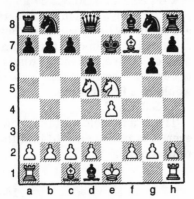

This position has been known for more than two hundred years. This is how the game between the French players de Legal and Saint-Brie, played in Paris in 1750, ended. Since then this finish is called **Legal's Mate**.

Exercises

(56) How strong (in numerical terms) is each player at the start of a game?

(57) White gave up a rook in return for a knight and three black pawns. To whose advantage is such a trade?

(58) Black gave up his bishop for three white pawns. Which side gained material?

(59) White took the queen in return for a rook, a bishop and a knight. Was he right?

(60) If a rook is given up for a bishop, how many pawns must be taken for the forces to be equalised?

155

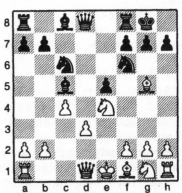

(61) Black to play. How would you continue?

The Third Period

Like a hockey match which is divided into three periods, a chess game is divided into three stages, the opening, the middlegame and the endgame. In the opening the opponents develop their pieces, mobilise all their men ready for the decisive battle, which takes place in the middlegame, and the endgame sums up the preceding struggle.

Not all games end with a direct attack on the king. More often than not, one of the players gets a material advantage, for example by winning a piece or a pawn. As a rule, such an advantage is realised only in the endgame, where an extra piece or pawn is especially significant. Therefore, exchanges are especially profitable for the player who has a material advantage.

Skill in the endgame is a great advantage to any player. Suppose that you have got a "numerical" advantage in one of the "periods" but do not know how to realise it. Then all your previous efforts would be in vain. The position you wanted to attain, believing it to be winning, may turn to be drawn or even losing. If you know typical positions and methods of realising a material advantage, you will avoid many disappointments.

When many exchanges leave few pieces on the board, it may turn out that the available forces are not sufficient for mating. Then a pawn becomes the principal character. Only a pawn can be promoted to a new piece and thus increase the strength of your army. In such cases the main goal is to promote a pawn to a queen and, when you have a queen, you must sensibly use it.

The role of the kings also becomes more important. In the opening and middlegame, when there are still many men on the board, the kings try to keep out of the enemy's sight since any piece can prove a danger. However, in the endgame, when the board becomes almost empty, the kings are in little danger and leave their hiding places to bravely join the last, decisive battle.

Imagine that, as the result of a devastating attack, one army is reduced to a king, minor piece and pawn while the other consists of a lone king. The aim of the first player is to promote his pawn to a queen. The last hope of the second player is to eliminate the final enemy pawn because it is impossible to give a checkmate with only a bishop or a knight.

To defend your pawn from an assault by the enemy king, you

should set up you pieces as shown in the following diagrams.

156

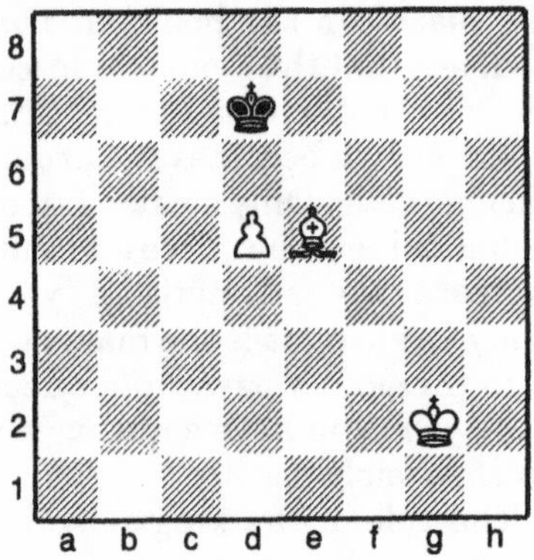

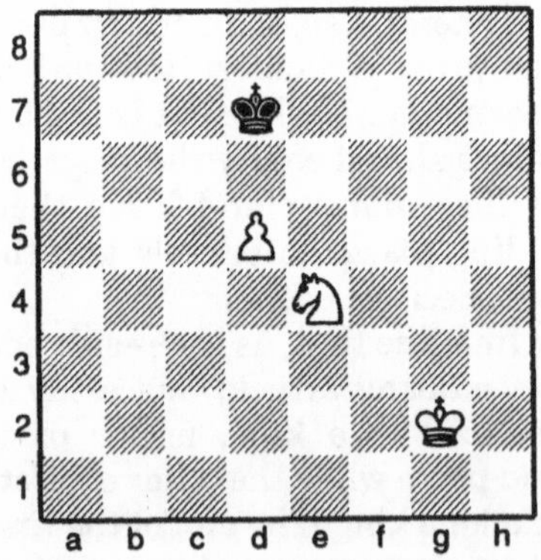

The black king cannot attack the pawn since all the squares in front of it are defended and a wide outflanking manoeuvre is too slow and, as we shall see later, quite useless.

157

Thus you have defended your pawn from a possible attack. However, it is hardly possible to promote it to a queen with the aid of a bishop or a knight alone, and so you will require the help of your own king.

Let us look at a possible continuation from diagram 156.

1 ♔f3 ♔e7 2 ♔e4 ♔d7 3 ♔d4 (the move 3 ♔f5 is also possible but it is more expedient to play with the king and the bishop from different sides) **3...♔e7 4 ♔c5 ♔d7 5 d6** (the pawn advances under the defence of the king and the bishop is free to do some other job) **5...♔d8 6 ♔c6 ♔e8 7 d7+ ♔e7** (if Black plays 7...♔d8, then White replies 8 ♗f6 mate). Now White queens his pawn, either with the support of his king, by 8 ♔c7 and 9 d8♕ or with the support of the bishop, by 8 ♗c7 and 9 d8♕.

There is no more trouble with the knight (diagram 157).

1 ♔f3 ♔e7 2 ♔f4 ♔d7 3 ♔e5 ♔e7 4 d6+ ♔d7 5 ♔d5 ♔d8 6 ♔c6 ♔c8 7 ♘c5 ♔d8 8 ♘b7+ (8 ♘e6+ is also possible) **8...♔e8 9 d7+ and 10 d8♕.**

In less favourable positions the main concern is the safety of the pawn.

In diagram 158 the black king wants to capture the d5-pawn, but White plays ♗e6 and then the pawn and the bishop protect each other.

158

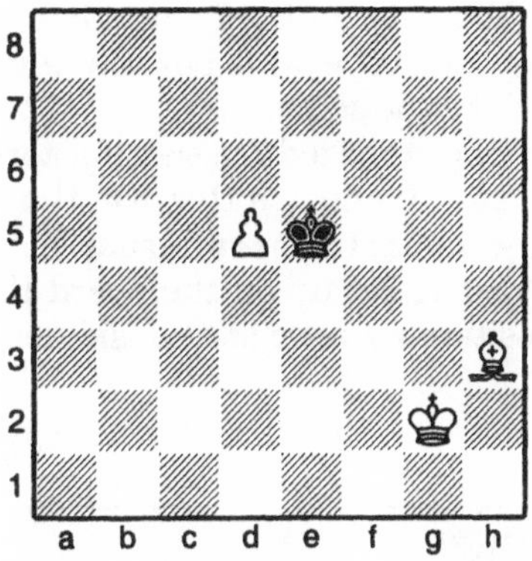

the latter will quickly run along the file to be queened, since the king has no time to catch up with it (verify it yourself!). Hence the bishop is **indirectly defended** and the white king can quietly approach the battlefield.

The knight has more subtle problems to solve.

160

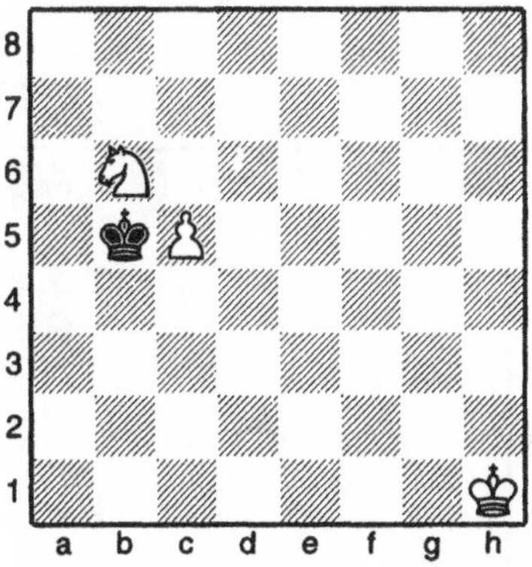

159

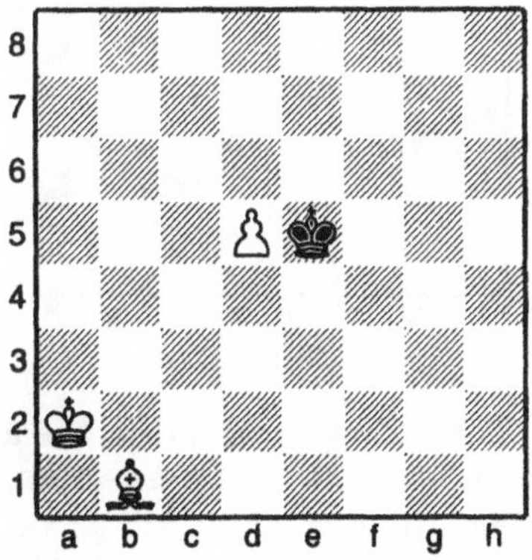

The position is similar to the preceding one, but here the white king prevents its bishop from defending the pawn on a2. The only solution is for the bishop to sacrifice itself by **♗e4**. Now the black king cannot capture the pawn and if it takes the bishop, then it will find itself behind the pawn and

The knight is defended by the pawn but the latter may perish and if is removed from the board, the position will be drawn. Suppose we defend the pawn: **1 ♘d7 ♚c6**. The king attacks the knight and the pawn at the same time. The knight cannot escape and the white king has no time to get to the scene of action, as after **2 ♚g2 ♚xd7 3 ♚f3 ♚c6** the pawn perishes.

The best move is **1 ♘a4!** Here, too, the knight defends the pawn but, unlike the preceding line, the black king cannot capture it since in that case it will get behind the pawn, **1...♔xa4 2 c6**, and White's pawn will be promoted to the queen.

Conclusion: **it is best for a knight to support an advancing pawn from the rear**.

Up till now we spoke of rules. These rules have some exceptions when there is an edge pawn (i.e., a-pawn or h-pawn).

161

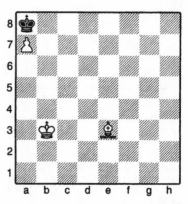

White has a material advantage and, in addition, his king supports the pawn. Nevertheless, the position is drawn because the dark-squared bishop cannot drive the enemy king from the light-squared corner. If we try, for example by **1 a6 ♔b8 2 ♔b6 ♔a8**, then White can at most stalemate the enemy king by **3 a7** or **3 ♗f4**. Alternatively, **1 a6 ♔b8 2 a7+ ♔a8** and any attempt to approach

the pawn with the king also ends in stalemate and, hence, a draw.

You can put any number of pawns on the a-file but the result will be the same.

One of the old Russian masters, Fyodor Ivanovich Duz-Khotimirsky, liked to lay unusual bets. Once he set up on the board the position we have just considered.

162

"I bet that I can queen the a7 pawn," he said to the spectators around him.

They all laughed heartily. The bet seemed to be ridiculous, but one gullible chess player decided to punish the maestro for his joke.

"I accept the bet. This is impossible."

Then Fyodor Ivanovich played **1 ♔b4** and asked the opponent to play Black.

"And where is your queen?" the latter asked ironically, replying

1...♔b7.

"Here it is," answered the master and, moving his pawn to a8, substituted the queen for it.

"But I shall immediately capture it with my king!" the opponent exclaimed.

"That was not the bet," Duz-Khotimirsky smiled.

The decision was unanimous: Fyodor Ivanovich won the bet.

Reverting to our subject, we have to point out that if we replace the dark-squared bishop by a light-squared one, we shall easily win.

163

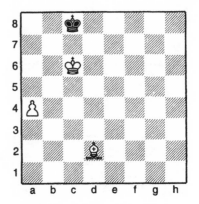

1 ♔b6 ♔b8 2 a7+ and after **2...♔a8** the game ends with a mate, **♗f3**, and in case of **2...♔c8** White gets a new queen, not as Duz-Khotimirsky did, but permanently!

Conclusion: **when you have an edge pawn, it is best to have a** **bishop moving on the same coloured squares as the corner promotion square**. If you have the 'wrong' bishop, then try to prevent the enemy king from reaching the corner in front of the pawn.

164

After **1 ♗f4** the black king is cut off from a8 and the pawn is promoted, but if Black is to play, then his king forces his way past b8 to the corner and the game is drawn.

When you have a pawn on the edge, you may also fail to win when you have a knight.

In diagram 165 the knight is tied to the defence of the pawn and any attempt to approach it with the king leads to stalemate.

Therefore, in diagram 166, you should not advance the pawn too quickly to a7, i.e. not **1 a7+?? ♔a8.** Instead you should first move

Exercises

165

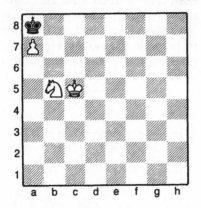

167

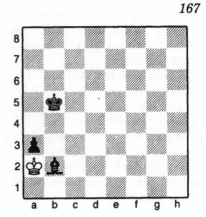

(62) Black to play. Find the easiest way to victory.

166

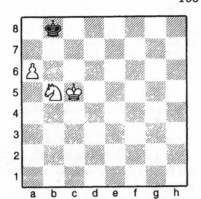

your king closer, and then your pawn can be easily queened: **1 ♔b6 ♔a8 2 ♘c7+ ♔b8 3 a7+ ♔c8 4 a8♕+.**

168

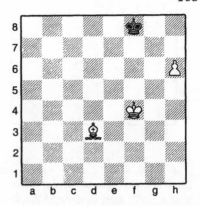

(63) How White can win on his move? (Two solutions.)

169

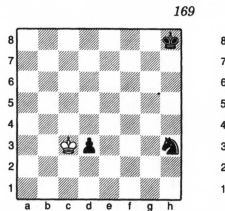

170

(64) Black to play. How would you play?

(65) White to play and win.

The Soul of Chess

The role of humble pawns is very significant in all stages of a chess game. Thus, the great French master of the 18th century André Danican Philidor called them the "soul of chess". In pawn endgames, when there are no other men on the board except the kings, they become the main force.

Chess players say that the shadow of a pawn ending hovers over every position. Why? Because exchange follows exchange during the game, pieces vanish one after another, and it is very important to estimate in advance the situation when only kings and pawns remain on the board.

"Ah, I Could Not Catch It!"

When a king and a pawn struggle against a lone king, you can gain victory only if you promote the pawn to a queen. Whether this is possible depends on the position of the pieces and sometimes on who is to play.

Can the black king stop the h3-pawn promoting? A novice begins to count moves bending fingers as an additional precaution: he moves there, I move here, he there, I here... And he runs the risk of losing count. I once knew an old man who played chess for forty years and every time when

he missed the chance of catching a passed pawn with his king, he exclaimed in distress: "Ah, I could not catch it!" He always hoped to catch up with it...

Remember that the **Rule of the Square** exists precisely for such positions.

If the king on its move can enter the square one side of which is the line extending from the pawn to its queening square then it can catch the pawn.

In our example the side of the square is the distance between the square h3 and the square h8. In order to construct a square, you should mentally draw a line along a diagonal connecting two opposite corners as shown in the diagram. Then you will see at once that it is sufficient for the black king to enter one of the squares on the file c3-c8 in order to catch up with the pawn h3. With Black to play, this is possible: **1...♚c4 2 h4 ♚d5 3 h5 ♚e6 4 h6 ♚f7 5 h7 ♚g7**. White's pawn is caught and therefore the game is drawn.

The square of the pawn diminishes with every move but the black king manages to stay within the square.

If, in the above diagram, White is to play, then the black king "misses the train" and the pawn easily queens. Let us verify this: **1 h4 ♚c4 2 h5 ♚d5 3 h6 ♚e6 4 h7 ♚f7 5 h8♕**. Black was one move too late.

Remember that on its first move, the pawn can advance two square at once; you must take this into account when you construct the square for a pawn on the second rank. For instance, if, in our example, the white pawn was on h2, then its battle against the enemy king would have been the same as with the pawn on h3.

The fight "for the square" sometimes becomes a key feature of play in a pawn ending.

Let us analyse the most well-known and the most instructive study on this subject. It was composed by the famous Czechoslovakian Grandmaster Richard Réti in 1922 and aroused general admiration.

White to play and draw.

172

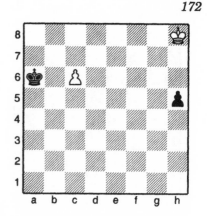

At first sight this seems to be impossible. The white king is far behind the black pawn on h5 which will not mark time but run as fast as it can to the promotion square on h1. It can be seen by the naked eye that even the Olympic Games sprinter will not catch up with it. On the other hand, the black king will easily catch the white pawn on c6 if the latter tries to force its way to c8.

All the same White makes a draw. He gains time with his king by threatening to support his pawn and thereby gets into the square of the enemy pawn.

1 ♔g7 h4 2 ♔f6! (diagram 173) White tries to kill two birds with one stone. If Black plays 2...h3, then the king will suddenly turn to the other side, **3 ♔e7!** and will help the white "bird" to promote, for example: **3...h2 4 c7 ♚b7 5 ♔d7 h1♕ 6 c8♕+** or **3...♚b6 4**

173

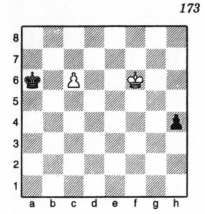

♔d7 h2 5 c7 h1♕ 6 c8♕. In both cases new queens spring up one after another, and this leads to a complete equilibrium of forces and a draw.

2...♔b6 3 ♔e5!

174

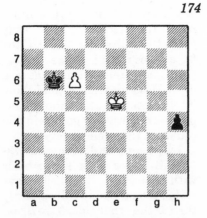

White is again ready to support his pawn: 3...h3 4 ♔d6 h2 5 c7

♔b7 6 ♔d7. At the same time his king is very close to the square of the enemy pawn.

3...♔xc6 4 ♔f4

White's king ceremonially enters the square and easily catches its prey.

4...h3 5 ♔g3

Now the game is drawn since only the kings will be left on the board.

How did that happen?

We are accustomed to consider a straight line to be the shortest distance between two points. The movement of the white king in Réti's position illustrates a special chessboard geometry, namely, **that the distance in a straight line is equal to the distance along a zigzag line**. This is because distances on a chessboard are measured not by a ruler but by moves. In the starting position (diagram 172) the white king can enter the square of the h5-pawn by 13 different routes each of which requires the same number of moves, namely, three. For instance, 1 ♔h7 2 ♔h6 3 ♔xh5 in a straight line, or 1 ♔g7 2 ♔h6 3 ♔g5 along a zigzag line (find the other routes).

Practical conclusion: **when necessary you can move your king along a zigzag line rather than along a file or a rank**.

It was precisely this peculiarity of the chessboard that helped the white king to catch up with the black pawn in Réti's position.

Here is an assignment for limbering-up.

176

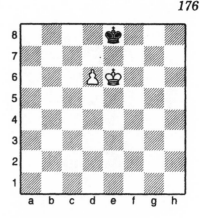

175

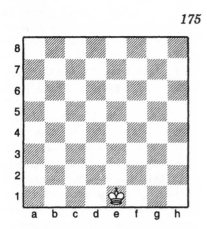

White to play, draw.
Black to play, White wins.

It is easy to calculate that moving along the e-file the white king will reach the square e8 in seven moves, but it can also reach the square e8 in the same seven moves – don't be surprised! – along 392 other routes! Try to compete with your friends: who will find and write down more routes in five minutes.

Which Is Better?

In most pawn endings the path of a passed pawn is blocked by the enemy king. This is a serious but not always insurmountable obstacle. Here is the main position to which pawn endings of this type reduce. The result of the position depends on whose turn it is to move.

White wins only with Black moving first: **1...♔d8 2 d7 ♔c7 3 ♔e7**, and the pawn, supported by the king, is promoted to a queen.

However, when White moves first the game is drawn: **1 d7+ ♔d8**, and, in order not to lose the pawn, White has to continue **2 ♔d6** stalemating the black king; this, as we know, means a draw.

In the above diagram White can try more subtle moves, for example **1 ♔e5 ♔d7 2 ♔d5** (diagram 177). This is a very important moment. Black must be very careful. If he retreats to c8 or e8 with his king, then, after **3 ♔c6** or **3 ♔e6**, he will again have diagram 176 but this time with Black to play, and this means his defeat.

2...♔d8! is a good move, after which Black is ready to meet the

177

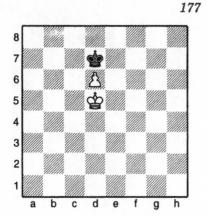

enemy king, depending on its move: if **3 ♔c6**, then **3...♚c8**, and if **3 ♔e6**, then **3...♚e8**, with a draw in both cases.

It is useful to know the following rule for positions of this type: **the pawn can be queened if it gets to the last rank but one without a check.**

You remember, of course, that when the kings face each other with a single square between them as in diagram 176, they are said to be **in opposition**. In such a position the kings cut each other off from the largest number of squares and, like two stubborn rams facing each other on a narrow bridge, do not let the other one pass.

The ancient Greeks used to say that it was better to stand than to go, it was better to sit than to stand, and it was better to lie than to sit... Most likely it was from laziness rather than wisdom. Wooden kings cannot be accused of laziness, but when they are in opposition they would prefer to stay put rather than budge from their places since a move by either king necessarily lets the other pass. Alas, according to the rules of chess, a player cannot skip his turn.

If, in diagram 176, it is Black's turn to play, then we say that **White has the opposition** and, *vice versa*, if it is White's turn to play, then **Black has the opposition**. In the present example, the outcome of the battle depended on this. It is not necessary to be a Greek in order to infer that it is better to have than to not to have.

Suppose now that, from diagram 177, we transfer the men several ranks downwards.

178

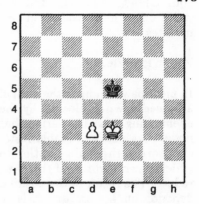

This is a draw irrespective of who is to play.

To be sure of defending, you must know that a lone king should stay in the path of a passed pawn until the enemy king takes its place beside it, and then you should take the opposition.

1 d4+ ♔d5 2 ♔d3 ♔d6 3 ♔c4 (it is the right moment for the black king to take the opposition) **3...♔c6! 4 d5+ ♔d6 5 ♔d4 ♔d7 6 ♔e5 ♔e7!** (again the enemy king meets an obstacle) **7 d6+ ♔d7 8 ♔d5.**

For a player who has an extra pawn it is better to keep his king in front of his pawn as this gives him the greatest winning chances.

to a queen irrespective of who has the opposition.

With Black to play: **1...♔e8 (c8) 2 ♔c7 (e7)**, and the pawn is free to advance to d8.

With White to play: **1 ♔e6 (c6) ♔e8 (c8) 2 d6**, and diagram 176 occurs with Black to move (2...♔d8 3 d7 ♔c7 4 ♔e7, White wins).

Why did the opposition of the kings in position 179 not save Black even when it was White's turn to play? The answer is that the reserve move with the pawn, 2 d6, allowed White to take the opposition at the decisive moment.

If the pawn has not yet reached the fifth rank, then the result depends only on who is to play.

179

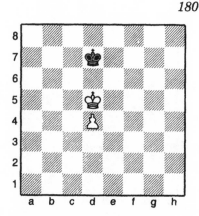

This diagram is a win irrespective of who is to play.

If the pawn has reached the fifth rank, with the supporting king in front, then it is promoted

180

White to play: Draw.
Black to play: White wins.

Let us first analyse the position when White is to play: **1 ♔e5 ♔e7**

2 ♔d5 ♚d7 3 ♔c5 ♚c7 (note that
the black king all the time keeps
the opposition, not yielding an
inch of the board to the opponent;
White is forced to either mark
time or move the pawn) **4 d5 ♚d7
5 d6 ♚d8! 6 ♔c6 ♚c8**. Now we
have a draw like the one in diagram 176.

However, if it is Black's turn to
play, his king has to give way and
White wins: **1...♚e7 2 ♔c6** (White
would reply to 1...♚c7 with 2 ♔e6)
**2...♚d8 3 d5 ♔c8 4 d6 ♚d8 5 d7
♚e7 6 ♔c7** and the pawn promotes.

If we transfer the pawn from
d4 to d3 in diagram 180, then
White wins whoever moves first.

181

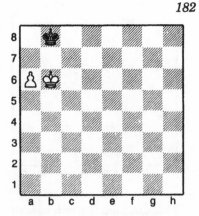

**A win irrespective of who
moves first.**
Playing 1 d4, White transfers
the move to the opponent and
takes the opposition.

Practical advice: **it is best to
keep your king in front of
your own pawn and manoeu-
vre it so that you can always
use the reserve move of the
pawn and take the opposi-
tion.**

The Edge Pawn

All the eight pawns are as similar
as twins but their behaviour is
not always the same. The edge
pawns have a peculiar fate. They
"live" in restricted conditions, on
the extreme files "a" and "h", and
no piece, either friendly or enemy,
can outflank them since they are
at the edge of the board.

How does this "one-sidedness"
affect the behaviour of the pawns?

182

**This is a draw irrespective
of who is to play.** With any other
pawn the outcome of the fight

would depend on who has the op-position. In a similar position (diagram 176) Black lost when it was his turn to play. Here, after 1...♔a8 2 a7, stalemate occurs and the game is drawn. The edge of the board does not allow White to force the king out of the corner it occupies.

183

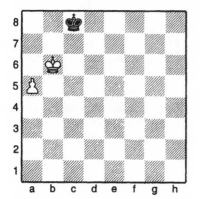

A draw irrespective of who is to play.

Black to play continues 1...♔b8 and draws as in the preceding example.

What happens if it is White's turn to play and he cuts the enemy king off from the corner square?

1 ♔a7 ♔c7 (diagram 184)

This is a draw irrespective of who is to play.

The black king sets up a blockade keeping the attacking king pinned to the edge of the board.

184

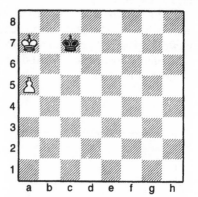

2 a6 ♔c8 3 ♔a8 (or 3 ♔b6 ♔b8) 3...♔c7 4 a7 ♔c8.

185

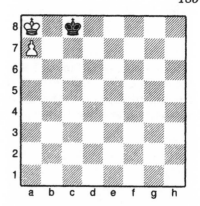

White has no legal moves – it is stalemate and therefore a draw.

Practical conclusion: **to stop the rook's pawn queening, it is sufficient for a lone king to occupy the square c8 as in** diagram 183 (or the squares c1, f1, f8 respectively).

If the square c8 (c1, f1, f8) is inaccessible to the lone king, the pawn is given a "green light" and it is easily promoted behind the shelter of its king.

186

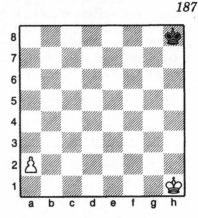

White to play continues **1 ♔b7**, preventing the black king from moving to c8, and promotes his pawn to a queen (verify this).

Exercises

187

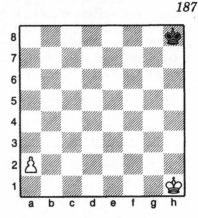

(66) Without moving the pieces, say how the game will end with White and with Black to play.

188

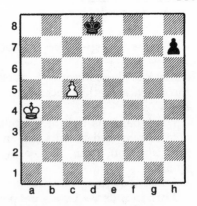

(67) White to play and draw. Hint: remember Réti's study (diagram 172).

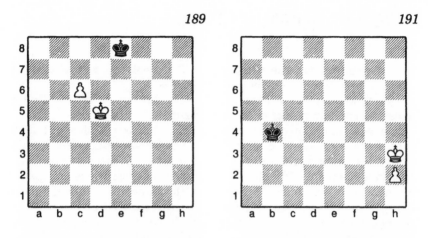

189

191

(68) White to play and win (two solutions).

(70) How will the game end (a) with White to play, (b) with Black to play?

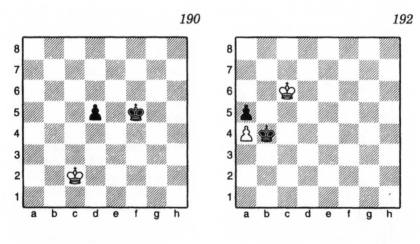

190

192

(69) Black to play and win.

(71) White to play and draw.

The Ubiquitous Queen

In the remote past, the rules of chess differed fundamentally from the game we play today. Then the queen was an unremarkable piece, which could move only to an adjacent square along a diagonal. Centuries passed before it occurred to someone: "What is the main duty of the queen?" Suddenly everybody understood that the queen was a loafer. The latter repented and promised to do the work of two from that time on.

It kept its word. Acting both as a bishop and as a rook, the queen can suddenly appear at the most distant scene of action, causing panic in the enemy ranks.

193

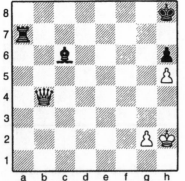

When it is White to play, he can win any one of Black's pieces.

The rook: **1 ♕b8+ ♔h7 2 ♕xa7+**.

The bishop: **1 ♕c3+ ♔h7 2 ♕xc6**.

The rook or the bishop: **1 ♕b6**.

The bishop or the pawn: **1 ♕d6**.

In each of these episodes the queen attacked two enemy pieces at the same time. This is known as a **double attack** or a **fork**. It is a favourite weapon of the queen, which is a long-range piece capable of all-round shooting. Any undefended piece could be the object of a double attack. **The aim of a double attack is to capture one of the men, i.e. to gain a material advantage**.

A double attack is especially efficient when the enemy cannot defend both pieces with a single move. If, for instance, in position 193 White plays 1 ♕d4+, it is a double attack since the queen simultaneously attacks the king and the rook. In this case Black will reply with 1...♖g7 defending his king and at the same time removing the rook from the queen's fire. Here the double attack missed its goal.

A double attack can be set up by preliminary moves.

In the following diagram the white queen does not yet possess a square from which it could simultaneously attack Black's king

194

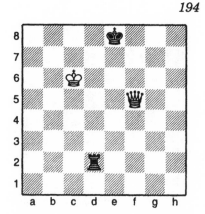

and rook. However, after **1 ♕e5+ ♚d8** it obtains such a square, namely, **2 ♕g5+**. If, on the other hand, Black plays either **1...♚f8** or **1...♚f7**, a double attack can be executed with **2 ♕f4+**. In both cases White wins the rook.

Sometimes a double attack is preceded by a sacrifice.

195

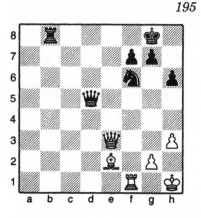

Black's position is rather strong, as he has an extra pawn, but there is a weak point in his ranks, the unprotected rook on b8. In general, it is not obligatory for all men to defend one another, but unprotected pieces must be watched carefully since they are vulnerable to a double attack.

1 ♖xf6! gxf6

Sacrificing the rook for the knight, White has cleared the way to the king and created one more target in Black's camp.

2 ♕g3+

This move is the double attack, on the king and the rook. White captures the rook on b8 and ends up with an extra bishop.

Note that in the case of 1...♖b1+ (instead of 1...gxf6) White would reply 2 ♖f1 blocking the check and removing the rook from the attack of the g7-pawn.

While attacking the king, the queen can successfully co-operate with other pieces. In diagrams 51-54 you got acquainted with some patterns where the principal force of the mating mechanism was the queen.

In the following five diagrams we can see how such mating positions arise in typical game situations. The first diagram shows queen and rook working together, in the following two it is queen and bishop, while in the final two the queen and knight go through their paces.

196

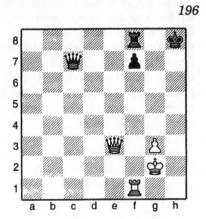

1 ♖h1+ ♔g7 2 ♕g5 mate.

198

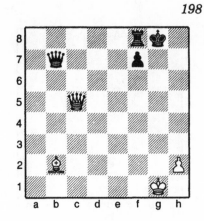

1 ♕g5+ ♔h7 2 ♕g7 mate.

197

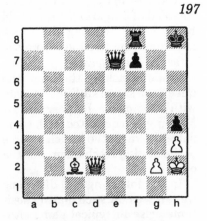

1 ♕h6+ ♔g8 2 ♕h7 mate.

199

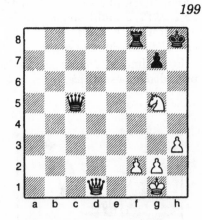

1 ♕h5+ ♔g8 2 ♕h7 mate.

200

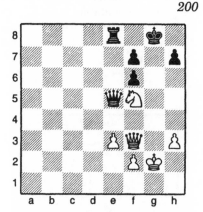

1 ♕g4+ ♔f8 (h8) 2 ♕g7 mate.

In all the examples given above White checkmated in two moves. Let us analyse the behaviour of the pieces. On its first move, one of the white pieces checked the black king. Black had a choice of at most two possible replies, so White could easily foresee what would happen. In each case Black was **forced** to move his king. To force means to drive, to compel. A **forced variation** leaves few, if any, choice of moves to the opponent.

A forced variation can be short or long. Former world champion Alexander Alekhine once said that in one of the games he had calculated a variation 20 moves ahead. It stands to reason that his calculation was simplified by the fact that every move of the opponent was forced.

How can forced variations be calculated? You must first define the aim you want to reach.

201

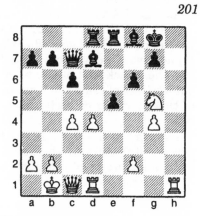

Let us analyse this position. White is attacking on the kingside, but the rook on the h-file does not threaten the enemy king. If it was the queen on the h-file instead of the rook, the move ♕h7 would be mate. This suggests the idea of moving the queen in the direction of the main attack.

With the move 1 ♕c2 (threatening 2 ♕h7 mate) White does not achieve his object. Black captures the knight on g5 (1...fg) and in the case of 2 ♕h7+ he can move his king to f7. White must think of a tactical device that would, first, allow him, to retain the knight on g5 and, second, not give time for Black to organise the defence of his king. The problem can be solved by the sacrifice of two rooks:

1 ♖h8+! ♔xh8 2 ♖h1+ ♔g8 3 ♖h8+! ♔xh8 4 ♕h1+

The queen has replaced the rook on the h-file and on the next move strikes the decisive blow.

4...♔g8 5 ♕h7 mate.

Note that the whole operation was conducted by checks. Black's replies were completely forced and the attack was played without any loss of tempo. Variations of this kind can be easily calculated.

Playing "with tempo" does not necessarily mean with checks; attacks and threats of other types can serve just as well.

2 ♕h6, and mate with the queen on g7 is unavoidable.

In this mating pattern White's bishop can be successfully replaced by a pawn.

203

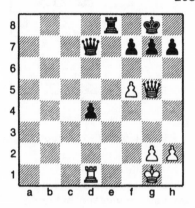

1 f6 g6 2 ♕h6, and mate on the next move.

202

1 ♗f6 (employing the pin of the g7-pawn, White attacks it with his bishop and queen, threatening mate on g7) **1...g6** (the only defence, but now "holes" have appeared in Black's camp; the queen immediately makes use of them)

Exercises

204

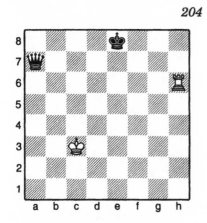

(72) Black to play. Think of a double attack (two solutions).

206

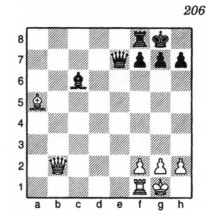

(74) Black to play. Can he win the white bishop?

205

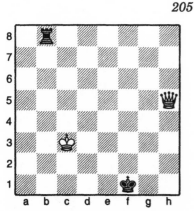

(73) White to play. Win the rook in three moves (three solutions).

207

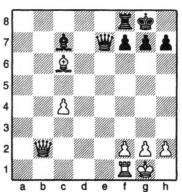

(75) And here?

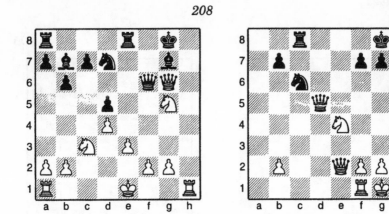

208

209

(76) White to play. Mate in two moves.

(77) White to play. Win the rook for your knight.

The Rook's Hour

At the start of a chess game, the main line of defence is formed by pawns. They are on the alert for enemy scouts. The pieces stand ready to support the actions of the pawns. The rooks are poised on the left and right edges of the board.

When marching orders are given, the first to move are the pawns. They are the first to fight and the first to suffer losses. Pawn exchanges result in the opening of lines; a file free of pawns is called an **open file**. Such a file frequently becomes the main direction of attack.

Now the rook's hour arrives. It is very important to seize open files with the rooks – like tanks, they can make deep raids to the enemy's rear.

In the following absolutely symmetrical position the player who is the first to occupy the open b-file gains an advantage.

Suppose that it is White's turn to move. He plays 1 **Rb1** and Black cannot prevent the rook from moving to b7, and then one of the pawns is lost, for instance after 1...a5 2 **Rb7** **Rc8** 3 **Ra7**.

The aim of seizing an open file is to penetrate into the enemy camp.

Here is how Mikhail Botvinnik prepared and carried out such a

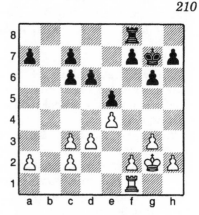

210

penetration in a game he played against Viktor Goglidze in 1935.

211

Black has an open c-file but wants to bring the other rook into the attack, since the more pieces that participate in the attack, the more effective it is.

1...Rab8!

Attacking the queen, Botvinnik seizes one more open file. Now both black rooks can participate fully in the game.

2 Wd6

White's first rank is defended only by the rook on f1. Black can easily remove this obstacle by sacrificing his queen.

2...Wxf1+! 3 Rxf1 Rb1+ 4 Re2 Rc2 mate

The distribution of chess pieces is such that the main reserves are usually concentrated on the seventh (last but one) rank. A rook penetrating onto this rank can reap a rich harvest; two are even better...

212

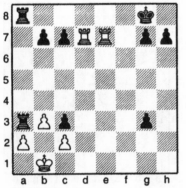

The two white rooks are on the 7th rank. In this position their

strength is doubled and, if White is to play, they can eliminate all six black pawns.

1 Rxg7+ Rf8 2 Rxh7 (the rook not only captures the pawn but also threatens checkmate on h8; Black has no time for active actions, he must organise a defence) **2...Rg8** (trying to run to the other side would cost Black dear after 2...Re8 3 Rxc7 Rd8 4 Rcg7, and mate next move) **3 Rdg7+ Rf8 4 Rxc7** (again a threat of mate and again the king must return) **4...Rg8 5 Rcg7+ Rf8 6 Rxb7** (the repeated manoeuvres of the rook are like the motion of a shuttle in a loom; every time the oscillations become greater and the number of black pawns decreases) **6...Rg8 7 Rbg7+ Rf8** (the rooks have run riot in the enemy's rear and can now concern themselves with the outlying pawns) **8 Rxg3** (at last Black has some respite) **8...Rxa2** (diagram 213)

It is important to play without mistakes as Black also has doubled rooks on the a-file and is ready to attack. If, for instance, White carelessly plays 9 Rxc3??, he will be mated in two moves: 9...Ra1+ 10 Rb2 R8a2#. Therefore, before capturing the pawn, White should swap one pair of rooks and make his king secure.

9 Rh8+ Rf7 10 Rxa8 Rxa8 11 Rxc3

Now White is two pawns up. This material advantage is sufficient to win.

213

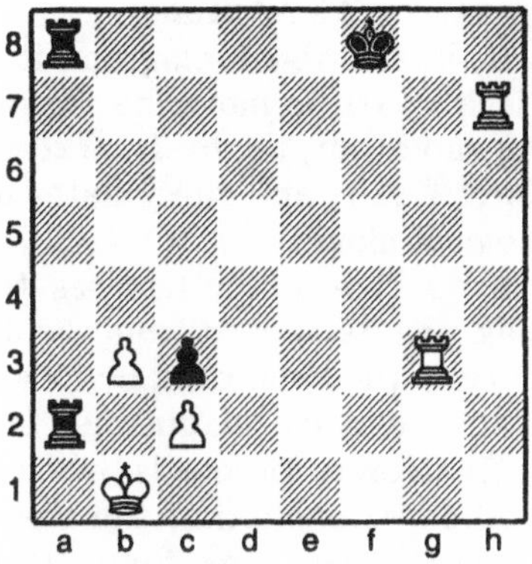

214

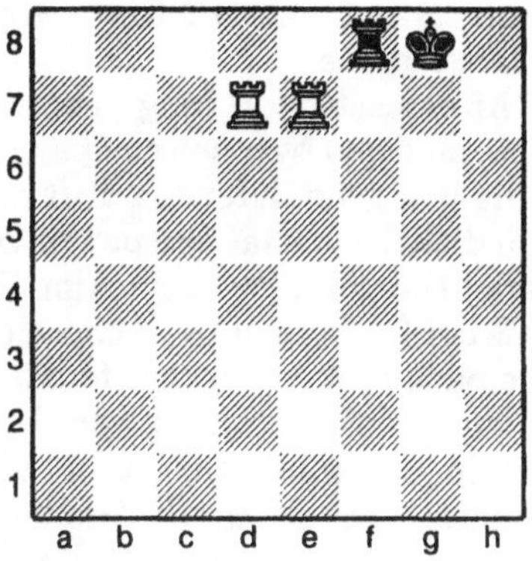

Let us return to diagram 212 and suppose that Black moves first. Then he can play **1...♖xa2** and the threat of checkmate on a1 enables him to defend. After **2 ♖xg7+ ♔f8** White cannot waste time (3 ♖xh7??) and he must be satisfied with perpetual check which means a draw: **3 ♖gf7+ ♔e8 4 ♖fe7+ ♔f8 5 ♖f7+ ♔g8 6 ♖g7+** and so on. This perpetual check is a common outcome of a rook attack on the seventh rank.

The combined action of two rooks frequently leads to checkmate. Diagram 214 shows one of the patterns:

White checkmates in three moves: **1 ♖g7+ ♔h8 2 ♖h7+ ♔g8 3 ♖dg7 mate**. The black rook on f8 cuts off the king's escape.

The position from diagram 215 is taken from a game played by the eminent 19th-century American player Paul Morphy (White).

215

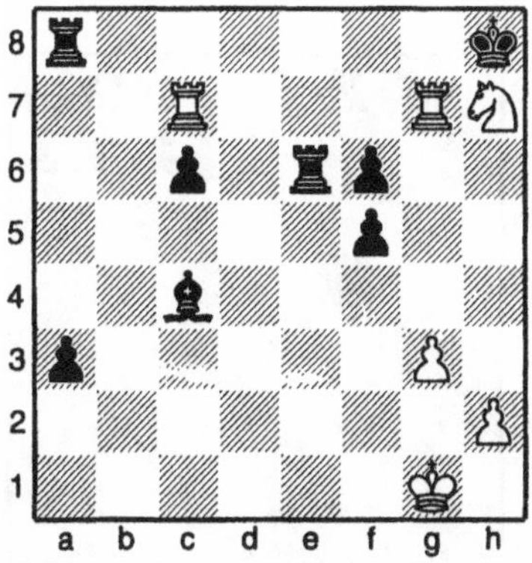

All Black's pieces on the seventh rank have been eliminated, but in the meantime Black had advanced his a-pawn which he wants to promote to a queen. White takes aim at his main target, the black king.

1 ♘f8! (the threat of 2 ♘g6# forces Black to capture the impertinent knight, but then his own rook moves to f8 and blocks his king's escape route, just as in diagram 214) **1...♖xf8 2 ♖h7+ ♔g8 3 ♖cg7 mate**.

After castling a king is at the side, shielded by a fence of pawns. This is a good defence but it has the drawback that the pawns restrict the mobility of the king. In this confined position, a check on the back rank may prove fatal.

The rook is the piece best suited to exploit this, as it can penetrate to the rear of the enemy along an open file and strike the decisive blow.

♖xc5, and only now, when Black's rook has left its post, White's rook can strike: **2 ♖d8 mate**.

If, in the above diagram, it is Black's turn to move, he wins in the same way, i.e. by **1...♛xd4 2 ♖xd4 ♖c1+**, and checkmates on the next move.

Note that in both cases the rook was **deflected** from the defence of the back rank by means of an exchange of queens. **The deflection of pieces** is the main method of exploiting the weakness of the last rank, for example by means of sacrifices.

216

217

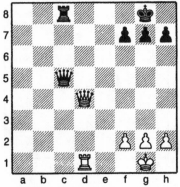

White to play. The eighth rank is defended by the rook, but perhaps the aim can be reached by means of a queen sacrifice, 1 ♛d8+? No, it cannot, since Black replies 1...♖xd8 2 ♖xd8+ ♛f8 (or at once 1...♛f8) and beats off the attack. The correct move is 1 ♛xc5

The doubled black rooks have taken aim at the square e1, but this square is defended by two white pieces, the queen and the rook. The attacking and defending forces balance. However, the move 1...♛c2! deflects one of the pieces from its duties. However

White takes the intrusive queen, he is checkmated on the first rank. The only other reasonable move, 2 ♗f4, is followed by a second queen sacrifice, 2...♕xc1+ 3 ♕xc1 ♖e1+, followed by mate on the next move.

In order to safeguard your king on the back rank, you must make an escape hatch for it, i.e. move one of the pawns in front of the king.

218

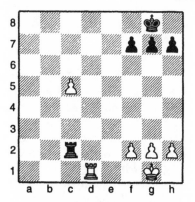

Black to play. He cannot take the c5 pawn since White threatens mate with the rook on the eighth rank, so he should make an **escape hatch** by 1...h6 or 1...g6 (he can also play 1...♔f8). Now the black king is safe and, in case of a check on d8, he can quietly move away. As to the white king, it has no escape so the white rook cannot leave the first rank. After 2 g3 or 2 h3, Black captures

the c5-pawn and restores material equality.

The great Spanish writer Miguel Cervantes made his hero Don Quixote fight with windmills. The result was deplorable. The poor knight was hooked by a vane of the windmill and thrown to the ground. To fight against a **chess 'mill'** is also a dangerous business. It can grind everything that gets in its way. The mechanism of the mill is put into effect, as a rule, by the combined actions of a rook and a bishop.

219

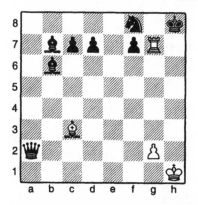

Note the position of the white rook and bishop with respect to the black king. The mill is already constructed. Here is how it works:

1 ♖xf7+

This is not a simple check but a **discovered** check. The rook moved but did not attack the king directly; instead it uncovered an attack from the bishop on c3 which was lying in ambush. After capturing the pawn, the rook is attacked by the queen on a2, but the queen cannot capture the rook since Black must first of all respond to the check.

1...♔g8 2 ♖g7+ ♔h8

All the pieces have returned to their places, but Black has lost a pawn. The whole process starts again from the beginning.

3 ♖xd7+ ♔g8 4 ♖g7+

This is similar to the shuttling of the rook in diagram 212.

4...♔h8 5 ♖xc7+

The millstones continue to grind and the black pieces perish one after another.

5...♔g8 6 ♖g7+ ♔h8 7 ♖xb7+ ♔g8 8 ♖g7+ ♔h8 9 ♖a7+ ♔g8 10 ♖xa2

White has ground everything he can and now has a decisive material advantage.

Two conditions are necessary for the work of the mill, namely the bishop must not be under attack and it must be impossible to block the diagonal along which it checks by enemy pieces. If, for instance, in the above diagram the queen is moved from a2 to c4, then, after 1 ♖xf7+, Black destroys the mill by either 1...♕xc3 or 1...♗d4.

In practice, it is sometimes possible to create the mechanism of the mill by means of a combination, as happened in the famous game the Mexican Grandmaster

Carlos Torre (White) played against Emanuel Lasker in 1925.

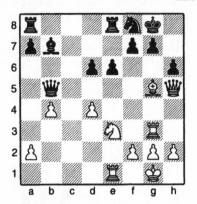

220

1 ♗f6!! ♕xh5 2 ♖xg7+ ♔h8 (White has sacrificed his queen, but now the positions of the rook and the bishop exactly correspond to the mill construction) **3 ♖xf7+ ♔g8 4 ♖g7+ ♔h8 5 ♖xb7+ ♔g8 6 ♖g7+ ♔h8 7 ♖g5+** (it is time to win back the queen) **7...♔h7 8 ♖xh5** and White went on to win (after **8...♔g6 9 ♖h3 ♔xf6 10 ♖xh6+** White stays three pawns ahead).

Exercises

221

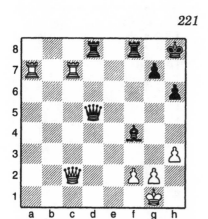

(78) White to play. What must be done (but watch out for the back rank mate)?

223

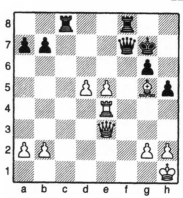

(80) Black to play. 1...♕f1+ is met by 2 ♕g1 and White has defended his pieces. Is there any other way for Black to conduct his attack?

222

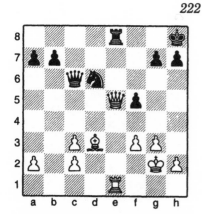

(79) White to play. The rook on e8 seems to be safely defended by the queen and knight. However...

224

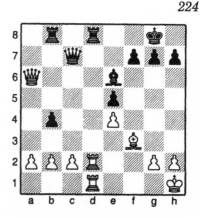

(81) White to play. Can the black queen be deflected from defending the rook on d8?

225   *226*

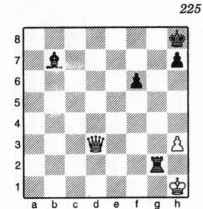

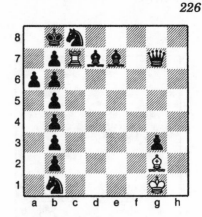

(82) The rook threatens to win the queen with a discovered check. Can White, to play, save his queen?

(83) In this odd position, can you successfully pass an examination to become a "miller"?

A Chameleon

The chess knight has a rather dubious reputation. It is sometimes called a "chameleon", because it changes the colour of the square it stands on at every step, sometimes a "despicable buffoon" of the chessboard, and, in general, it is regarded as a piece alien to noble society. All this because of its unusual move which some unknown inventor gave it.

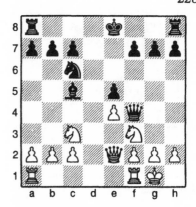

1 ♘e5!!
Ten black kings are mated at once! This can happen only in a frightful dream, but even in reality, the knight's behaviour is unceremonious.

1 ♘d5 (the knight has used the tactical device known as a double attack, as it has attacked the queen on f4 and the pawn on c7 simultaneously) **1...♕g4** (the queen must be saved first since it is the more important piece) **2 ♘xc7+** (again a double attack, the king and the rook on a8 are attacked at the same time; Black has no choice) **2...♔e7 3 ♘xa8 ♖xa8**.

White has won a rook and a pawn in return for the knight and thereby gained a decisive material advantage.

Double attacks with the knight are also known as knight **forks**. At the start of a game, when castling has not yet occurred, the rooks on a1 and a8 suffer most from knight forks, as in diagram 228.

In many cases a fork is prepared by an introductory sacrifice. Such forks are easy to overlook.

Lessons in Chess

229

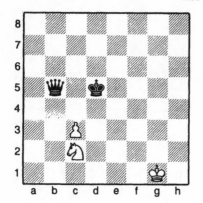

230

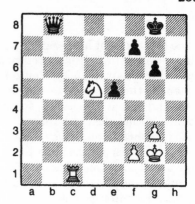

231

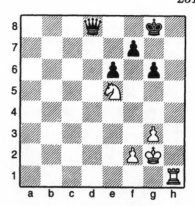

There is no fork yet, but in skilful hands...

1 c4+!

The pawn is sacrificed in order to entice the king or the queen to a square where both these pieces will be attacked by the c2-knight. After the continuation **1...♔xc4 2 ♘a3+** or **1...♕xc4 2 ♘e3+** Black loses his queen for a knight and a pawn, and this is to White's advantage.

The **enticement** of an enemy piece to a disadvantageous position often precedes a knight fork.

In diagram 230, the knight can only attack the king from e7 or f6. Sacrificing his rook, White forces the queen into the knight's firing range.

1 ♖c8+! ♕xc8 2 ♘e7+ and **3 ♘xc8**.

In diagram 231, the black king is enticed with the same aim in view.

1 ♖h8+! ♔xh8 2 ♘xf7+ and **♘xd8**.

Other pieces, too, can sacrifice themselves for the sake of a fork, as in diagram 232.

1 ♗b5! (the bishop has pinned the queen; in order to avoid losing the queen to the bishop, Black has to capture it) **1...♕xb5** (the queen

232

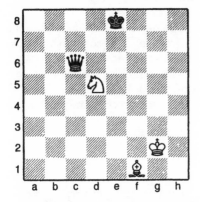

233

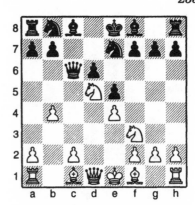

is precisely on the square where the knight wants it to be) **2 ♘c7+** and **3 ♘xb5**.

A combination of this kind can also occur at the very beginning of a game.

1 d4 c5 2 dc ♛a5+ 3 ♘c3 ♛xc5 4 e4 e5 5 ♘f3 d6 6 ♘d5 ♘e7?

Black has made mistakes in the opening. He developed his queen too early, allowing the white knight to consolidate its position in the centre. His last move was the decisive error.

7 b4! ♛c6 (diagram 233)

The queen has only one square to move to since all. the other squares are under the attack of White's pieces. Had Black played 6...♝e6 (rather than the mistake 6...♘e7?) on the previous move, he would now be able to retreat the queen to c8, preserving the possibility of defence.

Now you must mentally discard all the superfluous pieces and only recall diagram 232.

8 ♝b5! ♛xb5 9 ♘c7+ and **10 ♘xb5**

White has won the queen for a bishop.

One of the games of the World Championship played by Tigran Petrosian (White) and Boris Spassky in 1966 ended with a knight fork (see diagram 234).

After **1 ♘xf7 ♛xe3** White would be a pawn up, but the outcome of the game would not be clear because of the unreliable position of White's king. Petrosian found the best route to victory.

1 ♛h8+! (the king is deflected from the defence of the rook and is enticed to the h8 square where it is vulnerable to a knight fork) **1...♚xh8 2 ♘xf7+**. Now White wins back the queen and emerges a piece up.

234

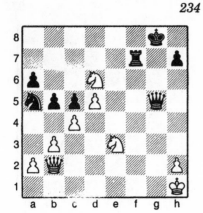

One of the most remarkable combinations is connected with the knight.

235

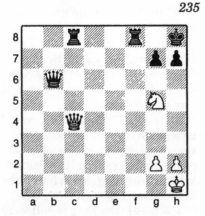

White's position seems to be absolutely hopeless. He is threatened with mate on b1, his queen on c4 is under attack and, in addition, Black has a great material advantage. Nevertheless, White wins if he is to play.

1 ♘f7+ ♚g8

The move 1...♖xf7 is impossible because of 2 ♕xc8 with checkmate in two moves. After 1...♚g8, however, if White gives a discovered check by 2 ♘d6+, then the black rook on c8 simply takes the queen.

2 ♘h6+!

236

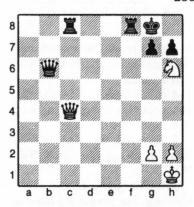

The two white pieces are both under attack but neither of them can be taken because they are both checking the enemy king. This type of attack, which is known as a **double check**, is very dangerous because the **only defence to a double check is a king move.**

2...♚h8

Now we can see a remarkable finish.

3 ♕g8+!! ♖xg8 4 ♘f7 mate!

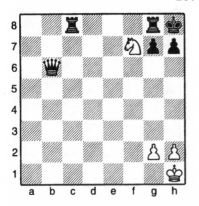

237

Black threatens checkmate on b2 and the rook on h1 is under attack. The queen on g2 defends the b7-pawn, so the attempt to attack the enemy king by 1 ♕e7+ proves to be useless after 1...♔b8. Nevertheless, White finds a way to attack the enemy king.

1 ♘b5+ ♔b8 2 ♕d6+! ♔a8

If 2...♖c7, then White should play not 3 ♕xc7+? ♔a8, but 3 ♕xf8+ ♖c8 4 ♕d6+ and so on as in the main variation.

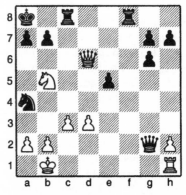

239

The queen has sacrificed itself in order to block the king in the corner. This combination is known as **smothered mate**. It has been known for 500 years but does not cease to be a delight for chess lovers.

Here is another example of the construction of a smothered mate:

238

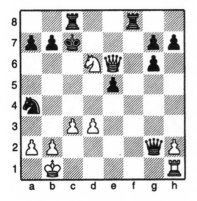

3 ♘c7+

The mechanism of the smothered mate begins to work. The move 3...♖xc7 is impossible due to 4 ♕xf8+. Is it clear now why, on the second move, the queen moved to d6 instead of taking the e5 pawn, again with a check? It did this in order to keep the rook on f8 under attack and thereby safeguard the white knight on c7.

3...♔b8 4 ♘a6+ ♔a8 5 ♕b8+ ♖xb8 6 ♘c7 mate.

Let us return to position 238 and see what happens if the king tries to escape to the other side of the board.

1 ♘b5+ ♔d8 2 ♕d6+ ♔e8 3 ♕xe5+ ♔f7 (playing 3...♔d7 does not help after 4 ♕d6+ ♔e8 5 ♖e1+ ♔f7 6 ♕e6 mate) **4 ♘d6+ ♔g8 5 ♕e6+** (again the queen moves to a square from which it attacks a rook, this time the other one) **5...♔h8 6 ♘f7+ ♔g8 7 ♘h6+ ♔h8 8 ♕g8+ ♖xg8 9 ♘f7 mate.** Smothered mate again, but this time in the other corner.

Even a discovered check involving the queen and the knight may bring trouble. Here is a mistake that beginners sometimes make at the very start of a game.

1 e4 e5 2 ♘f3 ♘f6 3 ♘xe5 ♘xe4?

It is not good to mimic White. The correct continuation is 3...d6 4 ♘f3 and only now 4...♘xe4 since to 5 ♕e2 Black can reply with 5...♕e7.

4 ♕e2 ♘f6??

This is suicide. After 4...♕e7 (or 4...d5 5 d3 ♕e7) 5 ♕xe4 d6 (the knight cannot retreat since the white queen is undefended) 6 d4 de 7 de, Black has only lost a pawn.

The opposition of White's queen and Black's king is dangerous. The knight which blocks the e-file can jump anywhere, discovering

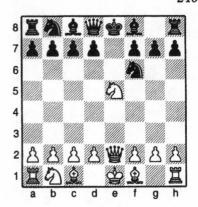

240

a check from the queen. Since Black must first of all deal with this check, he will have no chance to take the knight. White's knight must choose the most valuable target. For instance, White can play 5 ♘g6+ and the rook is eliminated after 5...♗e7 6 ♘xh8. However, there is an even bigger fish available...

5 ♘c6+!

White wins the queen and the game.

Exercises

241

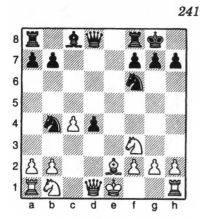

(84) White to play. Is the move 1 ♘xd4 a good one?

242

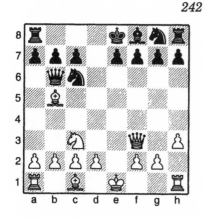

(85) White to play. How would you continue?

243

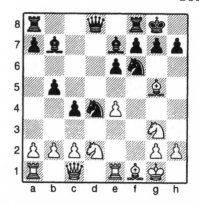

(86) White, the great Paul Morphy, is to move. What did the famous American play here?

244

(87) Black played 1...♘g4 and after 2 ♗xe7 continued with the surprising 2...♕b6!. White moved

his king away from the discovered check by 3 ♔h1. How did Black complete the combination?

245

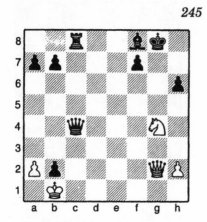

246

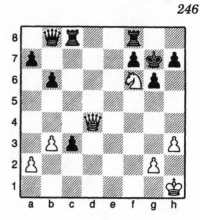

(89) And here?

(88) Black threatens mate on c1 but White, to play, has a discovered check. Which move is best?

The Opening: Questions and Answers

"Show me your shortest game," the former world champion Mikhail Tal was once asked.

"I am ashamed of recounting this," the grandmaster answered, feeling ill at ease, "but if you insist... I was nine years old and played against my elder brother:

1 e4 e5 2 ♗c4 ♗c5 3 ♕h5 ♘f6?? 4 ♕xf7 mate."

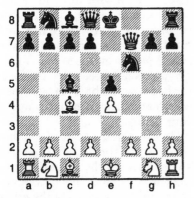

We will not say which of the brothers played White and which played Black.

Can we mate still quicker? We can:

1 e4 e5 2 ♕h5 ♔e7?? 3 ♕xe5 mate.

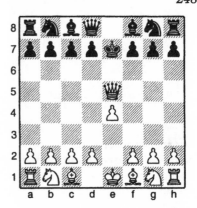

And quicker still?

Emanuel Lasker once watched a game between beginners. After 1 f4 e6 White asked:

"Tell me please, maestro, what is the best move now?"

"g2-g4," the World Champion answered at once.

"You have given me bad advice!" said White after the move 2...♕h4 mate (diagram 249).

"I meant that this move was the best ... for Black."

This is the shortest possible game. It is practically impossible to lose in less than two moves. However, there was a case once...

The Georgian master Archil Ebralidze was well known for his

249

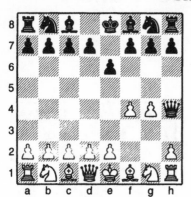

quarrelsome character. Once he came to a tournament and, after his opponent played 1 e4, he asked for the referee of the tournament.

"I resign," he said.

"Why?" asked the surprised referee.

"I don't like his face," said Ebralidze, pointing at his opponent.

Is it true? Many anecdotes are told about chess players, but quite a lot of them are apocryphal.

To avoid a fiasco on the very first moves, you must know the fundamental rules of the opening. Just as the construction of a building begins with the foundations, a chess game begins with the opening. The well-played opening creates conditions for a successful offensive and victory, but conversely, mistakes in the opening can lead to a quick and sudden defeat.

A chess player must remember three main principles in order to feel confident in the opening. By following them, you will be able to gain good positions even in unfamiliar opening variations.

The first principle is that of quick development of the pieces.

At the start all the pieces (except for the knights) are immobilised by their own pawns. To develop them, one needs time. **Time in chess is measured by moves (tempi)**. To spend time on moves that do not serve the purpose of development is the same as to mark time in a sprint after the starter fires his gun. Thus **you should not move the same piece twice; it is better to use the time to bring out another piece**. Do not move the rook's pawns on the a- and h-files when it is not necessary. It is better begin with the d- or e-pawns, whose advance opens the way for your pieces.

Remember: the more pieces that take part in the action, the more advantageous the squares that they occupy and the better are your chances to win. On the other hand, a premature offensive unsupported by sufficient forces often ends in defeat.

1 e4 e5 2 ♗c4 ♘f6 3 ♘f3 ♘xe4 4 ♘c3

White does not intend to win back his pawn. He makes the sacrifice intentionally, to develop his

250

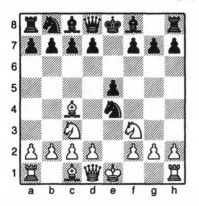

pieces as early as possible. After 4...♘xc3 5 dc White is appreciably ahead of his opponent in development since the knight on f3 and the bishop on c4 are already in fighting positions, files are open for the queen and the bishop on c1. In contrast Black, who has made three moves in a row with his knight, which vanished from the board as a result, has not yet developed a single piece. True, he is a pawn up.

A game in which one player sacrifices material in the opening for the sake of rapid development is called a **gambit**.

All the same, Black should have agreed to the continuation 4...♘xc3 since it would have led to an interesting struggle of White's better development against Black's extra material. Instead, he begins a dashing attack unsupported by sufficient forces.

4...♘xf2? 5 ♔xf2 ♗c5+

As chess players use to joke, nobody has yet died of a check.

6 d4!

White is true to his tactics. He is ready to give up one more pawn in order to be able to bring out new pieces.

6...ed 7 ♖e1+ ♔f8 8 ♘e4 ♗b6

251

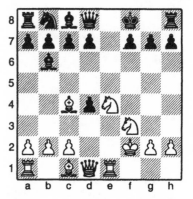

We see material equality on the board, in that Black has three pawns against the white knight. However, he is in a hopeless situation. Only the bishop on b6 is participating in the battle while White has mobilised almost the whole of his army and is ready to go on the offensive. One way to win is 9 ♗g5! f6 (or 9...♕e8 10 ♘d6, and Black loses the queen) 10 ♘xf6! gf 11 ♗h6 mate. White can also gain victory by other means since his advantage is so large.

9 ♕d3 d5 10 ♕a3+ ♔g8 11 ♗xd5 ♕xd5

White has sacrificed the bishop having in mind a beautiful final combination.

252

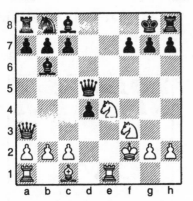

12 ♘f6+! gf 13 ♕f8+! ♔xf8 14 ♗h6+ ♔g8 15 ♖e8 mate.

This is how the lovers of "Blitzkrieg" are normally punished. A premature, poorly-prepared offensive is easily repulsed and then follows a decisive counterattack.

Beginners often make a mistake in the opening by developing the queen too early. The queen is the strongest piece but also the most vulnerable, since it should only be exchanged for the opposing queen. A thoughtlessly developed queen is subject to the attacks of less valuable pieces and has to lose time by moving again and again.

1 e4 d5 2 ed ♘f6 3 c4 c6

A gambit, i.e. Black offers a pawn sacrifice. It is better not to take the pawn, but to play 4 d4 and develop the pieces, but White goes badly wrong.

4 ♕a4? ♗d7 5 dc ♘xc6 6 ♕b3?

A "semi-repentance". The move 6 ♕d1 would be a complete admission of guilt, but it would be safer. Now White attacks the b7-pawn, thinking naively that Black will spend time on its defence, but Black's lead in development allows him to begin a decisive offensive.

6...♘d4! 7 ♕c3

7 ♕xb7 would be followed by a knight fork, 7...♘c2+, winning a rook.

7...e5 8 f4? ♗b4!

Black continues to attack the queen. With every move, Black improves the position of his pieces whereas White thinks only of his queen's safety.

9 ♕d3

9 ♕xb4?? is impossible because of 9...♘c2+.

9...♗f5!

There is no peace for the queen anywhere.

10 ♕g3 ♘e4!

Black could already have won the rook by 10...♘c2+, but he counts on much more.

11 ♕xg7 ♘c2+ 12 ♔e2

Out of twelve moves, White has made six with his queen and five pawn moves. Now he moves his king without touching any other

253

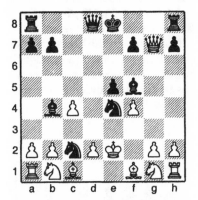

piece. While White has been wasting time, Black has brought out almost his whole army and saved his queen for a decisive blow.

12...♕d3+!! 13 ♔xd3 (13 ♔d1 ♘f2#) **13...♘g3 mate!**

254

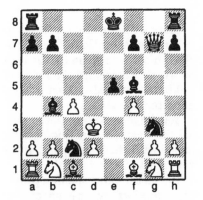

Certainly a remarkable position! All Black's four minor pieces are taking part in the mate and each of them controls squares adjacent to the enemy king.

Note that Black carried out his attack only through the centre. **The fight for the control of the centre** is the second opening principle.

Why is the centre so important? Because the pieces which are on central squares (or which control central squares) are more mobile and possess the greatest striking power. They can be quickly transferred to either side of the board as necessary.

Here is the famous game played by Edward Lasker and Sir George Thomas in 1912 in which White's **centralised pieces** work wonders.

1 d4 e6 2 ♘f3 f5 3 ♘c3 ♘f6 4 ♗g5 ♗e7

It would be better to play 4...d5 to prevent the opponent from gaining control of the centre.

5 ♗xf6 ♗xf6 6 e4 fe 7 ♘xe4 b6 8 ♘e5 ♗b7 9 ♗d3 0-0 10 ♕h5

White has created the threat of 11 ♘xf6+ ♖xf6 12 ♕xh7+ ♔f8 13 ♕h8+ ♔e7 14 ♕xg7+, winning. It could have been easily prevented by the exchange 10...♗xe5.

10...♕e7 (diagram 255)

Now to 11 ♘xf6+ Black replies with 11...gf and the queen protects the h7-pawn from e7. However, Edward Lasker carries out a stunning combination, ideally illustrating the strength of centralised pieces.

255

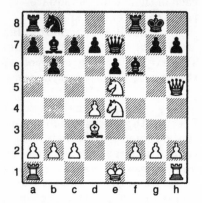

11 ♕xh7+!!

The most valuable piece is given up for only a pawn.

11...♔xh7 12 ♘xf6+

The double check drives the king out into the open. There is no way back, as 12...♔h8 allows 13 ♘g6 mate.

12...♔h6 13 ♘eg4+ ♔g5

256

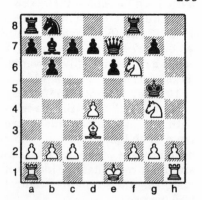

All Black's moves are forced and the king soon meets its death.

14 h4+ ♔f4 15 g3+ ♔f3 16 ♗e2+ ♔g2 17 ♖h2+ ♔g1

Not long ago the black king was quite safe on its throne under the guard of its servants, but now it has to die surrounded by enemies.

18 ♔d2 mate!

257

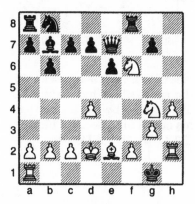

Mate with the king! A situation deserving attention! True, the checkmate was given by the rook on a1, and therefore the move 18 0-0-0 mate was also possible. It is a matter of taste.

You have certainly noted that all the examples in this chapter ended with checkmate, and at the very start of a game at that.

Hence the third opening principle: **look after the safety of your king**.

You should try to develop your pieces as soon as possible and clear the way for castling in order to hide the king in the least dangerous position at the side of the board. If the king gets stuck in its starting position (e1 or e8), it is subject to attack.

Here is an example from a game played by Alexander Alekhine (White) in which a delay in castling proved to be fatal for his opponent.

1 e4 e6 2 d4 d5 3 ♘c3 ♗b4 4 ♗d3 ♗xc3+

This exchange was not necessary. It would have been better to play 4...de 5 ♗xe4 ♘f6 6 ♗f3 0-0.

5 bc h6?

Moves which are time-wasting, such as this one, are said to involve a loss of tempo. They should be avoided in the opening. Here it would be better to play 5...de 6 ♗xe4 ♘f6 and 7...0-0.

6 ♗a3!

258

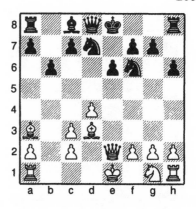

The bishop has been brought out to a superb position from which it hinders castling. Black needs to expend a great deal of effort to move his king to a safe place.

6...♘d7 7 ♕e2 de 8 ♗xe4 ♘gf6?

It would be correct to play 8...♘e7, thereby closing the diagonal of the bishop on a3 and preparing for castling although, due to his earlier mistakes, Black's position would still be very difficult.

9 ♗d3 b6?

Black does not notice the threat, although it is difficult to give him any good advice since his opening was very poor. Perhaps only 9...c5 would have saved him from immediate defeat.

259

10 ♕xe6+! fe 11 ♗g6 mate.

The king was taken prisoner before he had time to resign.

The pawn on f7 (or on f2, respectively) is one of the most vulnerable points in the starting position since it is defended by the king alone and, until castling occurs, it is exposed to attack, which can have very serious consequences.

1 e4 c6 2 d4 d5 3 ♘c3 de 4 ♘xe4 ♗f5 5 ♘g3 ♗g6 6 h4 h6 7 ♘f3 ♘d7 8 ♗c4 e6 9 ♕e2 ♗d6 10 0-0 ♘gf6 11 ♘e5 ♗h7?

It stands to reason that Black had to prevent an exchange on g6 since in the case of, say, 11...0-0 12 ♘xg6 fg the pawn on e6 would be without defence. However, Black should have played 11...♗xe5 12 de ♘d5 followed by castling, but now White destroys the defence of the enemy king by means of a typical sacrifice.

After castling, the square f7 must still be carefully guarded from possible attacks.

1 e4 e6 2 d4 d5 3 ♘c3 de 4 ♘xe4 ♘d7 5 ♘f3 ♘gf6 6 ♗d3 b6 7 0-0 ♗b7 8 ♕e2 ♗e7 9 ♖e1 0-0 10 ♘eg5 ♖e8?

In contrast to the preceding example, Black had time to castle but he has carelessly left the f7-pawn without sufficient defence.

261

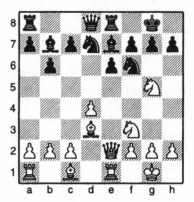

11 ♘xf7! ♗xf3 12 gf ♔xf7 13 ♕xe6+ ♔f8 14 ♗c4, and checkmate on f7 can only be averted by large material losses (14...♘e5 15 de ♕d5 16 ♗xd5).

Even after castling, the king is still not left in peace; not only f7, but also h7, may be subjected to attack.

1 e4 e6 2 d4 d5 3 ♘c3 ♘f6 4 ♗g5 ♗e7 5 ♗xf6 ♗xf6 6 e5 ♗e7 7 ♗d3 c5 8 dc ♗xc5 9 ♕g4 0-0 10 ♘f3 ♘c6?

260

12 ♘xf7! ♔xf7 13 ♕xe6+ ♔g6 (f8) 14 ♕f7 mate.

10...f5 would have been correct.

262

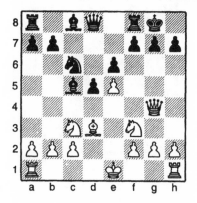

11 ♗xh7+! ♔xh7 12 ♕h5+ ♔g8 13 ♘g5 ♖e8

Black tries to prevent the mate on h7 but he is doomed to failure.

14 ♕xf7+ ♔h8 15 ♕h5+ ♔g8 16 ♕h7+ ♔f8 17 ♕h8+ ♔e7 18 ♕xg7 mate

Memorise the mechanism of this combination. A bishop sacrifice on h7 (h2) is one of the most common methods of attacking a castled king, and is known as the **"Greek Gift"** sacrifice.

Exercises

1 e4 e6 2 d4 d5 3 ♘d2 c5 4 ed ed 5 dc ♗xc5 6 ♘e2??

263

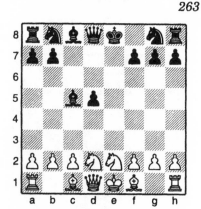

(90) Black to play. How would you continue?

1 e4 e5 2 ♘f3 ♘c6 3 ♗c4 ♗e7 4 d4 ed 5 c3 dc??

264

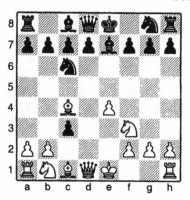

(91) White to play. How would you continue?

1 e4 e5 2 ♘f3 ♘c6 3 ♗c4 ♘f6 4 d4 ed 5 0-0 d6 6 ♘xd4 ♗e7 7 ♘c3 0-0 8 h3 ♖e8 9 ♖e1 ♘d7?

266

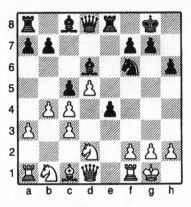

265

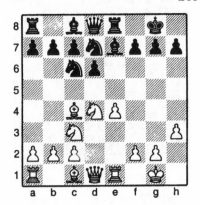

(92) White to play. How would you continue?

1 e4 e5 2 ♘f3 ♘c6 3 ♗c4 ♘f6 4 ♘g5 d5 5 ed ♘a5 6 d3 h6 7 ♘f3 ♗d6 8 c3 0-0 9 b4 ♘xc4 10 dc c5 11 a3? e4 12 ♘fd2 ♖e8 13 0-0? (see diagram 266)

(93) Black to play. How would you continue?

1 d4 d5 2 c4 e5 3 e3 ed 4 ed ♘f6 5 ♘c3 ♘c6 6 ♗g5 ♗e6 7 cd ♗xd5 8 ♘xd5? ♕xd5 9 ♗xf6? (see diagram 267)

(94) Black to play. How would you continue?

267

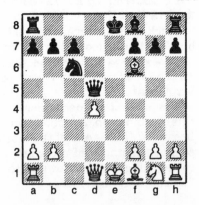

1 e4 d5 2 ed ♕xd5 3 ♘c3 ♕d8 4 ♘f3 ♗g4 5 ♗c4 e6 6 h3 ♗xf3 7 ♕xf3 c6 8 d3 ♕f6? 9 ♕g3 ♘h6 10 ♗g5 ♕g6 11 ♘b5 cb? (see diagram 268)

(95) White to play. How would you continue?

268

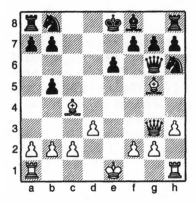

Check Your Solutions

(1) The square f7 is white. The squares b1, b2, b3, b4, b5, b6, b7 and b8. The diagonal h4-d8 includes five squares, namely, h4, g5, f6, e7 and d8. The squares a6, b6, c6, d6, e6, f6, g6 and h6.

(3) Black's position is ♔e8, ♕d8, ♖a8, ♖h8, ♗c8, ♗f8, ♘b8, ♘g8, ♙a7, b7, c7, d7, e7, f7, g7, h7.

(4) The squares f8, a1, g8, c2 and f2.

(5) The black king has only two squares to move to, namely, d5 and f4. The squares d6, e4, e6, f5 and f6 are attacked by the queen and the square d4 is attacked by the knight.

(6) The king can capture the knight on b3 or the c4-pawn. The rook is defended by the knight and the b4-pawn by the bishop.

(7) Yes, by playing the rook to a2.

(8) Yes, by playing the rook to g8 (but not to a2 since this square is under the attack of the knight).

(9) ♕g2-b2.

(10) ♕h6-f8 (but not to e3 since this square is under the attack of the bishop).

(11) d5-d6.

(12) In two moves, namely, b7-b6 (or b7-b5) and ♗c8-a6.

(13) The knight must start with the pawn on a6 and capture all the other pawns as follows: c5, b3, d2, f3, h4, g6, e7.

(14) Here are all the routes: ♘g1-f3-e5-f7-d8; ♘g1-f3-e5-c6-d8; ♘g1-e2-f4-e6-d8. You cannot play ♘g1-f3-g5 or ♘g1-f3-d4 since these squares are under the attack of the queen.

(15) Here is one of the possible routes: ♘h1-f2-d3-c1-b3-a1-c2-b4-a6-c7-a8-b6-d7-f8-g6-h8-f7-g5-e4-g3-h1.

(16) Not less than four moves. Here is one of them: ♘c3-e2-g1-f3-e5. There are many other routes, but it cannot capture the pawn in less than four moves. This position of the knight relative to the object which it intends to attack is the most disadvantageous.

(17) At least six moves. For instance, ♘d7-e5-d3-b4-d5-e3-f5 = 6 moves. It will need more time if it begins with the other pawn, namely, ♘d7-e5-f3-d4-f5-e3-d5-b4 = 7 moves.

(18) White can capture the black pawns on c6 and e6 with the d5-pawn and the f5-pawn with the g4-pawn; Black can capture the white pawn on d5 in two ways, namely, either with the c6-pawn or with the e6-pawn and he can capture the pawn on g4 with the f5-pawn. The black pawn on b4 can meet the move c2-c4 by capturing the white pawn *en passant*, moving the pawn to the square c3

in the process; White can reply to the move g7-g5 by capturing this pawn *en passant* from h5.

(19) There are eight possibilities, namely, (1) ♕b2, (2) ♘b2, (3) ♘e5, (4) ♗e5, (5) e5, (6) f6 and (7) ♖g7 and (8) ♔h7.

(20) If you defend the king by the queen on b8 or d8 or by the knight on c8 or e8, then the rook will simply capture the piece and keep attacking the king. The best move is ...♗g8 since the bishop will be defended by the king.

(21) ♕f6 mate.

(22) ♗h3 mate.

(23) ♕a7 mate.

(24) ♕e1 mate.

(25) ♕f8 mate.

(26) ♖h1 mate.

(27) ♘f3 mate.

(28) ♗e5 mate.

(29) Yes, ♖b7.

(30) Yes, ♗g2.

(31) Yes. After ♖b5 the knight is pinned. Black defends it by moving his pawn to d6, but then White plays d4 and on the next move takes the knight with the pawn.

(32) Yes. White plays f2-f4! If Black retreats with his king, then the rook becomes undefended and the bishop will take it. The only move that remains is g6-g5, but then White takes the pawn with his pawn, again attacking the rook which perishes since it is pinned by the bishop.

(33) ♕h3 mate, but not ♕h6+ since then White will play ♕h5.

(34) ♕e1 mate (the white queen is pinned by the g5 bishop).

(35) Only on the kingside as the white queen controls the square d8 and the black queen controls the square d1.

(36) Only on the queenside. When castling short, the white king moves into check from the bishop on c5. The black king's rook is on g8, and this means that it has already moved. The fact that the black queen's rook must pass through the square b8 that is under attack from the bishop is of no importance for castling long.

(37) White cannot castle at all since his king would have to pass through squares under attack, namely f1 when castling short and d1 when castling long. Black can only castle short. The fact that the rook on h8 is under the attack of the knight is of no importance for castling.

(38) White can do this in four ways, namely, ♗b5+, ♗g4, ♖d1 or 0-0-0. Black has only one way of doing this, namely, the bishop takes the g2 pawn.

(39) Although the black king has no vacant squares to move to, there is no stalemate since the g5-pawn has a legal move.

(40) Black is in stalemate, as neither the king nor the remaining pawns have any legal moves.

(41) The squares h1 and e1.

(42) White cannot immediately take the queen since then the black king will be in stalemate,

but if he first checks with the rook on h7, then, after ...♔g8, the black king will have a free square on f8 and White can take the queen. There is also another way of doing this, namely, to give up one rook by means ♖g8+ and then take the queen, remaining with an extra rook.

(43) Yes, he can. The black king is in stalemate, hence it is desirable to get rid of the rook. The rook is sacrificed by ...♖b1+, the white king does not take it (otherwise stalemate will follow) and moves to a2, but the rook continues chasing it by ...♖b2+, and so on until the king is tired of moving back and forth. A rook of this kind is called a desperado rook.

(44) White escapes by means of perpetual check by ♕g5+, then ♕d8+, again ♕g5+ and so on. It is incorrect to begin with ♕e8+ since after ...♔g7 the white queen cannot check any more and the sacrifice of the queen does not lead to stalemate because White has a pawn on a2 and can move it.

(47) White: ♔e1, ♕b3, ♖a1, ♖h1, ♗h6, ♘e2, ♙a2, b2, c2, d4, f2, g2, h2 (13). Black: ♔f7, ♕d8, ♖a8, ♖e8, ♗c8, ♗e7, ♘d7, ♙a7, b7, c6, f6, g6, h7 (13).

(48) White: ♘1xf2 or ♘3xf2, Black ♖axc7 or ♖gxc7.

(49) White: ♖1xb5 or ♖8xb5, Black ♘exf3 or ♘hxf3.

(50) 1 ♖h7 ♔f8 2 ♖d8 mate.

(51) 1...♖cb5 2 ♔a8 ♖a6 or 2...♖a5 mate.

(52) 1 ♕h7 ♔f8 2 ♖d8 mate.

(53) 1...♗b3 2 ♔a1 ♖c1 mate or 1...♖a8 2 ♔c1 ♖a1 mate.

(54) 1 ♕d5 ♔a6 2 ♕a8 mate, or 1...♔a4 2 ♕a2 mate; 1 ♕g2 ♔a6 2 ♕a8 mate, or 1...♔a4 2 ♕a2 mate; 1 ♕g8 ♔a6 2 ♕a8 mate, or 1...♔a4 2 ♕a2 mate.

(55) 1 ♗e2 ♔a7 2 ♗f2+ ♔a8 3 ♗f3 mate; 1 ♗c8 ♔a7 2 ♗f2+ ♔a8 3 ♗b7 mate.

(56) 39.

(57) To White's advantage as he is now the equivalent of a pawn up.

(58) Neither side. It was an even trade.

(59) No, he was not. The rook, the bishop and the knight cost as much as 11 pawns and the queen costs only 9 pawns.

(60) Two pawns.

(61) 1...♘xe4! 2 ♗xd8 (if you play 2 de, then 2...♕xg5 and Black wins a piece) 2...♗xf2+ 3 ♔e2 ♘d4 mate. This is Legal's Mate again.

(62) 1...♔b4 2 ♔b1 ♗e5 (but not 2...♔b3?? stalemate) 3 ♔a2 ♔a4 4 ♔b1 ♔b3 5 ♔c1 a2, and the pawn is queened.

(63) 1 ♗c4 ♔e7 2 h7, and the pawn is queened; 1 ♗h7 ♔f7 2 ♔f5 ♔f8 3 ♔f6 ♔e8 4 ♗g8 (or 4 ♔g7) 4...♔f8 5 h7, and the pawn is queened.

(64) The pawn must be defended from behind, i.e. by 1...♘f4. It is not good to play 1...♘f2? because then 2 ♔d2 ♔g7 3 ♔e3 ♔f6 4 ♔xf2 ♔e5 5 ♔e3, and the game is drawn.

(65) Black threatens to play his king to b5 and take White's last pawn. White should retreat with his knight to ensure the defence of the pawn, but where? Let us consider every possibility: (a) 1 ♘c7 (the moves 1 ♘c5 ♔xc5 2 a6 ♔b6 are senseless) 1...♔c5 2 ♔g2 (or 2 a6 ♔b6) 2...♔c6, and to any move of the knight Black replies with 3...♔b5 taking the pawn, (b) 1 ♘b8 ♔b5 2 a6 ♔b6 3 ♔g2 ♔a7 with the same result. The correct moves are (c) 1 ♘b4! ♔b5 (or 1...♔xb4 2 a6, and the pawn queens) 2 a6. The knight defends the pawn from behind and is, therefore, invulnerable. White moves up the king and wins as in diagram 166.

(66) Both with White to play and with Black to play the pawn queens since the black king does not have enough time to get into the 'square'. When Black is to play this occurs because the a2-pawn can move two squares on its first move.

(67) Moravetz's problem (1952). 1 ♔b5 h5 (if 1...♔c7, then 2 ♔c4 and the white king gets in the square of the h-pawn) 2 ♔c6! (with the threat of queening his pawn if 2...h4 3 ♔b7 h3 4 c6 h2 5 c7+ and so on) 2...♔c8 3 ♔d5, and the white king enters the square of the h5-pawn.

(68) 1 ♔e6! (setting up the opposition; 1 ♔d6? ♔d8 leads to a draw, as in diagram 176) 1...♔d8 2 ♔d6. There is also a round-about way, namely, 1 ♔c5 ♔d8 2 ♔b6 ♔c8 3 c7 (without check), and White wins.

(69) 1...♔e4 (1...♔f4? 2 ♔d3 is a draw) 2 ♔d2 ♔d4 3 ♔e2 ♔c3 4 ♔d1 ♔d3 5 ♔c1 ♔e2 6 ♔c2 d4, and the pawn queens.

(70) With Black to move, his king manages to get to the square f8 and draw: 1...♔c5 2 ♔g4 ♔d6 3 ♔g5 ♔e7 4 ♔g6 ♔f8.

White to play wins: 1 ♔g4 ♔c5 2 ♔g5 ♔d6 3 ♔g6 ♔e7 4 ♔g7, and the pawn marches to h8.

(71) It is impossible to defend the a4-pawn, but when the black king takes it, the white king must force it to the edge of the board as in diagram 184: 1 ♔d5 ♔xa4 2 ♔c4 ♔a3 3 ♔c3! (but not 3 ♔b5? a4 4 ♔c4 ♔b2 5 ♔b4 a3, and Black wins) 3...♔a2 4 ♔c2! a4 5 ♔c1 and the game is drawn.

(72) 1...♕e3+; 1...♕g7+.

(73) 1 ♕h1+ ♔f2 (e2) 2 ♕h2+ and 3 ♕xb8; 1 ♕f3+ ♔e1 (g1) 2 ♕g3+ and 3 ♕xb8; 1 ♕h3+ ♔e1 (g1) 2 ♕g3+ and 3 ♕xb8; 1 ♕h3+ ♔e2 (f2) 2 ♕h2+ and 3 ♕xb8.

(74) Yes, he can: 1...♕g5 threatens mate on g2 and at the same time attacks the bishop on a5.

(75) Yes, he can: 1...♕d6 with the same double attack.

(76) 1 ♖h8+! (the king is enticed to h8 and bishop cannot take the rook as it is pinned) 1...♔xh8 2 ♕h7 mate.

(77) 1 ♘f6+! gf (otherwise you lose the queen) 2 ♕g4+ and 3 ♕xc8.

(78) 1 ♕h7+! ♔xh7 2 ♖xg7+ ♔h8 3 ♖h7+ ♔g8 4 ♖ag7 mate.

(79) 1 ♕xd6! Black resigns. The move 1...♕xd6 is followed by 2 ♖xe8+ ♕f8 3 ♖xf8 mate and the move 1...♖xe1 is followed by 2 ♕f8 mate.

(80) 1...♖c1+! 2 ♕xc1 (2 ♕e1 ♕f1+) 2...♕f1+ 3 ♕xf1 ♖xf1 mate.

(81) It can, but there is only one move that works, namely, 1 ♕a7! Now 1...♕xa7 is followed by 2 ♖xd8+ ♖xd8 3 ♖xd8 mate. If 1...♕c8, then 2 ♕xb8 (or 2 ♖xd8+, also winning material) ♖d2 3 ♕xc8+ ♗xc8 4 ♖xd2, and White is a rook up; or 1...♖xd2 2 ♕xc7 ♖xd1+ 3 ♗xd1, and White gets a queen for a rook. The move 1 ♕c6? would be incorrect because of 1...♕xc6 (1...♕e7 is also possible) 2 ♖xd8+ ♕e8, and White gains nothing.

(82) He cannot. Wherever the queen moves, Black attacks it with the rook and at the same time gives a discovered check with the bishop. For instance, 1 ♕d8+ ♖g8+, 1 ♕d7 ♖g7+, 1 ♕b1 (b3, b5) ♖b2+, 1 ♕f1 ♖f2+ and so on (without the h3-pawn, White could save himself, if not the queen, by 1 ♕xh7+! ♔xh7 stalemate).

(83) 1 ♖xb7+ ♔a8 2 ♖d7+ ♔b8 3 ♖b7+ ♔a8 4 ♖xb6+ (it would be incorrect to play 4 ♖xe7+ ♔b8 since the rook cannot return to b7 because of 5...♕xb7, and 5 ♖xg7 ♘d6 not only destroys the mechanism of the mill but

also results in White's defeat) 4...♔a7 5 ♖b7+ ♔a8 6 ♖xb5+ (the rook has passed to the b-file and eliminates everything it meets) 6...♔a7 7 ♖b7+ ♔a8 8 ♖xb4+ ♔a7 9 ♖b7+ ♔a8 10 ♖xb3+ ♔a7 11 ♖b7+ ♔a8 12 ♖xb2+ ♔a7 13 ♖b7+ ♔a8 14 ♖xb1 ♔a7 15 ♖b7+ ♔a8 16 ♖xe7+ (now it can finish on the 7th rank) 16...♔b8 17 ♖xg7. Let us take a breath now. White has eliminated ten enemy pieces and will now take the 11th (pawn on g3) to end up a rook ahead. This is what the mill means!

(84) No, it is a bad one: 1 ♘xd4? ♕xd4! 2 ♕xd4 ♘c2+ and 3...♘xd4 and Black wins a knight for a pawn.

(85) 1 ♘d5! ♕a5 (if 1...♕xb5? or 1...♕c5, then 2 ♘xc7+) 2 b4! Now the queen has nowhere to go and must take the bishop on b5 (the knight on c6 is pinned), which is followed by a knight fork on c7.

(86) 1 ♕a3+ ♔g8 (1...♔e8 2 ♕e7#) 2 ♘e7+ ♔f8 3 ♘g6+! ♔g8 4 ♕f8+! ♖xf8 5 ♘e7 mate! It is one of the forms of a smothered mate.

(87) 3...♘f2+ 4 ♔g1 ♘e2+! 5 ♘xe2 (♗xe2) ♘h3+ 6 ♔h1 ♕g1+ and 7...♘f2 mate.

(88) You can win the queen: ♘e3 (e5)+ ♗g7 2 ♘xc4, However, after 2...♖xc4 White has no reliable defence to ...♖c1+. The correct move is 1 ♘f6+! Black can avert the double check only by 1...♔h8, but then 2 ♕g8 delivers mate.

(89) Here you might like to win the queen by 1 ♘d7+ ♚g8 2 ♘xb8, but then Black replies with 2...c2 and gets a new queen, and with check at that. The double check, 1 ♘h5+, does not give the desired result since Black play 1...♚h6 rather than 1...♚g8? 2 ♕g7 mate, and if 2 ♕g7+ ♚xh5 3 ♕xh7+, then 3...♚g5 and White has nothing to attack with. Victory can be achieved by means of another double check, namely, 1 ♘e8+! Now 1...♚g8 is met by 2 ♕g7 mate and 1...♚h6 by 2 ♕h4 mate.

(90) 6...♕b6, and the deadly threat 7...♗xf2 mate can only be repulsed at the expense of a piece (7 ♘d4 ♗xd4 8 ♕e2+).

(91) 6 ♕d5, and mate on f7 can only be prevented by a sacrifice of a piece (6...♘h6 7 ♗xh6 0-0).

(92) 10 ♗xf7+! ♚xf7 11 ♘e6! In order not to lose the queen, Black must take the white knight, 11...♚xe6, but then 12 ♕d5+ ♚f6 13 ♕f5 mate.

(93) 13...♗xh2+! 14 ♚xh2 ♘g4+ 15 ♚g3 (15 ♚g1 ♕h4) 15...♕d6+ 16 f4 (else 16...♕h2#) 16...ef+ 17 ♚xf3 ♖e3 mate.

(94) 9...♗b4+! 10 ♚e2 ♕e4 mate!

(95) 12 ♕xb8+! ♖xb8 13 ♗xb5 mate.

The Editor's Choice

A selection of the 10 of the best games played by

Garry Kasparov, World Chess Champion

and Chief Chess Adviser, Cadogan Books

Garry Kasparov, arguably the world's greatest-ever chess player, was born in Baku, the capital of Azerbaidzhan, on April 13th 1963. Learning to play chess at the age of six, he became a pupil of the legendary Russian Grandmaster Mikhail Botvinnik (three times World Champion) and impressed his trainer with his phenomenal memory, amazing tactical insight and powerful will to win.

These qualities, together with the iron discipline taught by Botvinnik and wisdom gained by learning from the great masters of the past, enabled Garry to rise rapidly through the ranks and become the youngest-ever World Champion (at the age of 22) in 1985.

Since then he has successfully defended his title five times, including three FIDE (World Chess Federation) matches against the former World Champion, Anatoly Karpov. In 1993 (now playing under the auspices of his own Professional Chess Association) Kasparov scored a decisive victory over England's Nigel Short and in 1995 he comfortably held off India's Vishy Anand.

Garry's playing style – classical, uncompromising and aggressive – makes him a favourite of chess fans everywhere, and his initiatives to popularise chess world-wide (including a televised speed chess Grand Prix, matches with chess computers and a teaching programme for schools) have brought the game to an ever-widening audience.

Here we present ten of Garry Kasparov's greatest chess games, full of incredible tactics, lightning attacks and imaginative ideas. These inspiring games are surely the most remarkable "Lessons in Chess" of all!

The Editor

Viktor Korchnoi –
Garry Kasparov
Lucerne Chess Olympiad,
Switzerland, 1982
Benoni Defence

269

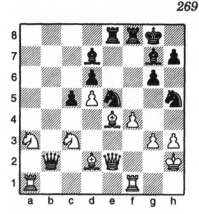

1 d4 ♘f6 2 c4 g6 3 g3 ♗g7 4
♗g2 c5 5 d5 d6 6 ♘c3 0-0 7 ♘f3
e6 8 0-0 exd5 9 cxd5 a6 10 a4
♖e8

Garry Kasparov – at the age of
19 playing the famous Viktor
Korchnoi, World Title Challenger,
for the first time – chooses the
sharp Benoni Defence to take on
his experienced opponent. White
will try to gain an advantage in
the centre by e4 (and eventually
e5 if possible) while Black aims to
use his extra queenside pawn by
advancing ...b5 at a suitable moment.

11 ♘d2 ♘bd7 12 h3 ♖b8 13
♘c4 ♘e5 14 ♘a3 ♘h5 15 e4 ♖f8
16 ♔h2 f5

It was fine for Black to continue his queenside play with
16...♗d7 and 17...b5, but the
young Kasparov is more ambi-
tious – he wants to attack on both
sides of the board!

17 f4 b5! 18 axb5 axb5 19
♘axb5 fxe4 20 ♗xe4

Korchnoi wisely refuses to take
the offered piece – this would be
met by either 20...♗xe5 or the incredible 20...♘xg3, blasting open
the white king's defences.

20...♗d7 21 ♕e2! ♕b6! 22
♘a3 ♖be8 23 ♗d2? ♕xb2!!

Only now did Korchnoi realise
that his intended 24 ♖fb1, to win
the queen, fails to the clever reply
24...♘f3+! Taken aback, he now
loses his way in the complications.
24 ♖a2, to eject the annoying black
queen, would have been sensible.

24 fxe5?! ♗xe5 25 ♘c4 ♘xg3!

270

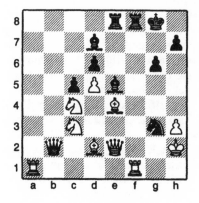

A stunning blow, which gives Black a winning advantage. Despite some inaccuracies on both sides, Garry eventually wins this very imaginative game.

26 &xf8+ &xf8 27 &e1 &xe4+ 28 &g2 &c2 29 &xe5 &f2+? 30 &xf2! &xf2 31 &a2! &f5! 32 &xd7 &d3 33 &h6? &xd7 34 &a8+ &f7 35 &h8? &f6 36 &f3?? &xh3+ White resigns.

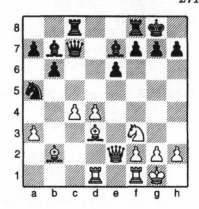

271

Garry Kasparov –
Lajos Portisch
Nikšić, Yugoslavia, 1983
Queen's Indian Defence

1 d4 &f6 2 c4 e6 3 &f3 b6 4 &c3 &b7 5 a3 d5 6 cxd5 &xd5 7 e3 &xc3 8 bxc3 &e7 9 &b5+ c6 10 &d3 c5 11 0-0 &c6 12 &b2 &c8 13 &e2 0-0 14 &ad1 &c7 15 c4 cxd4 16 exd4 &a5 (diagram 271)

White's two pawns at c4 and d4 are controlling lots of central squares, but are also coming under attack from Black's pieces. White's next move (a temporary pawn sacrifice) blows open the centre and allows the bishops to use their long-range power to attack the black king.

17 d5! exd5 18 cxd5 &xd5 19 &xh7+ &xh7 20 &xd5 &g8 (diagram 272)

Black's king looks quite safe again, but now Kasparov plays a brilliant long-term sacrifice to keep the king exposed.

21 &xg7!! &xg7 22 &e5!

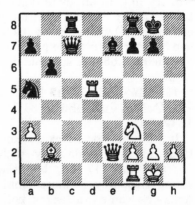

272

Another fine move! The knight is centralised, making way for the queen to join the attack at g4. There is no safe place for the black king to hide.

22...&fd8 23 &g4+ &f8 24 &f5 f6 25 &d7+ &xd7 26 &xd7 &c5 27 &h7 &c7 28 &h8+ &f7 29 &d3 &c4 30 &fd1 &e5 31

♕h7+ ♔e6 32 ♕g8+ ♔f5 33
g4+ ♔f4 34 ♖d4+ ♔f3 35 ♕b3+
The king has been chased all the
way up the board and now comes
to a sticky end. If 35...♕c3 then 36
♕d5+ leads to mate.
Black resigns.

Robert Hübner –
Garry Kasparov
*Hamburg Match,
West Germany, 1985*
English Opening

1 c4 e5 2 ♘c3 d6 3 d4 exd4 4
♕xd4 ♘f6 5 g3 ♘c6 6 ♕d2 ♗e6
7 ♘d5 ♘e5 8 b3 ♘e4 9 ♕e3 ♘c5
10 ♗b2 c6 11 ♘f4? ♘g4! 12 ♕d4
♘e4!!

273

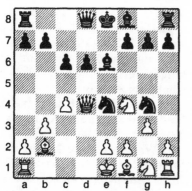

A bombshell. Black threatens
both a deadly check on a5 and to
take on f2. If White tries to cover
everything by means of 13 ♘d3

then 13...f5, with the idea of trap-
ping the queen by 14...c5!, is hard
to meet.

13 ♗h3 ♕a5+ 14 ♔f1 ♘gxf2
15 ♗xe6 fxe6 16 ♘xe6 ♔d7! 17
♘h3 ♘xh3
Instead of greedily capturing
the rook, when the knight would
be trapped in the corner, Kasparov concentrates on attacking the
king.

18 ♕xe4 ♖e8 19 ♘c5+ ♕xc5
20 ♕g4+ ♔c7 21 ♕xh3 ♗e7!
Rapidly mobilising pieces to
catch the king undefended.

22 ♗xg7

274

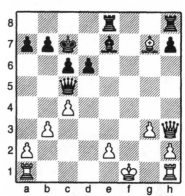

22...♖hf8+!
It's not a difficult decision for
Garry to sacrifice rook for bishop;
Black's three remaining pieces
are unopposed as they track down
the hapless monarch.

23 ♗xf8 ♖xf8+ 24 ♔e1 ♕f2+
25 ♔d1 ♕d4+ 26 ♔c2 ♕e4+ 27

♔d2 ♗g5+ 28 ♔c3 ♕e5+ **White resigns.**

Anatoly Karpov –
Garry Kasparov
World Championship Match,
Moscow, 1985
Sicilian Defence

1 e4 c5 2 ♘f3 e6 3 d4 cxd4 4 ♘xd4 ♘c6

This is one of the main lines of the Sicilian, Kasparov's favourite defence to 1 e4. Black exchanges his c-pawn for White's central d-pawn, gaining a 2-1 central pawn majority and a half-open c-file for his rooks. White, for his part, has a space advantage because of his pawn at e4 and slightly more active pieces.

5 ♘b5 d6 6 c4 ♘f6 7 ♘1c3 a6 8 ♘a3 d5?!

275

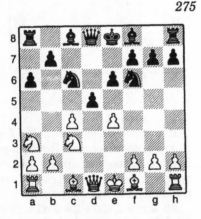

An amazing, if flawed, idea which shocked the chess world (and Anatoly Karpov!) at the time of the match. Kasparov's plan is to take advantage of the time wasted by the white knights to launch a central pawn sacrifice, freeing lines for his pieces. Afterwards the correct antidote was found, but at the board Karpov was unable to "bust" what Garry later called his "supreme creative achievement".

9 cxd5 exd5 10 exd5 ♘b4 11 ♗e2 ♗c5

Opting for active piece play rather than the immediate recapture of the d5-pawn. Karpov now misses his chance to play 12 ♗e3!, meeting 12...♗xe3 with 13 ♕a4+! and White gains the advantage. After the move played in the game, Kasparov's active pieces fully compensate for White's extra pawn.

12 0-0 0-0 13 ♗f3 ♗f5 14 ♗g5 ♖e8 15 ♕d2 b5 16 ♖ad1 ♘d3!

A very strong post for the knight, curbing the activity of the whole white army.

17 ♘ab1? h6! 18 ♗h4 b4! 19 ♘a4 ♗d6 20 ♗g3 ♖c8 21 b3 g5! 22 ♗xd6 ♕xd6 23 g3 ♘d7

If White's offside knight tries to re-enter the fray by 24 ♘b2, Black can spring a diabolical trap: 24...♕f6!! 25 ♘xd3 ♗xd3 26 ♕xd3 ♘e5! with a deadly knight fork on f3.

24 ♗g2 ♕f6 25 a3 a5 26 axb4 axb4 27 ♕a2 ♗g6 28 d6 g4! 29 ♕d2 ♔g7 30 f3 ♕xd6 31 fxg4

Wd4+ 32 ⌘h1 ⌁f6 33 ⌸f4 ⌁e4 34 Wxd3 ⌁f2+ 35 ⌸xf2 ⌁xd3 36 ⌸fd2 We3! 37 ⌸xd3 ⌸c1!!

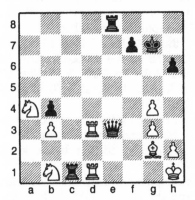

276

With bishop and two knights for the queen, Karpov seemed to be surviving, but this move snuffs out all resistance. If 38 ⌸xe3, then 38...⌸xd1+ wins too many pieces – White's back rank is a fatal weakness.

38 ⌁b2 Wf2 39 ⌁d2 ⌸xd1+ 40 ⌁xd1 ⌸e1+ White resigns.

Jeroen Piket –
Garry Kasparov
Tilburg, Holland, 1989
King's Indian Defence

1 d4 ⌁f6 2 ⌁f3 g6 3 c4 ⌁g7 4 ⌁c3 0-0 5 e4 d6 6 ⌁e2 e5 7 0-0 ⌁c6 8 d5 ⌁e7

The starting point for many of Kasparov's battles in the King's Indian. White will seek his chances on the queenside and Black will try to attack on the kingside. Many fine positional victories have been won from the white side, but when Black breaks through on the kingside it is more than likely to end in mate!

9 ⌁e1 ⌁d7 10 ⌁e3 f5 11 f3 f4 12 ⌁f2 g5 13 b4

The race begins in earnest!

13...⌁f6 14 c5 ⌁g6 15 cxd6 cxd6 16 ⌸c1 ⌸f7 17 a4 ⌁f8 18 a5 ⌁d7! 19 ⌁b5?! g4 Kasparov has purposefully left out the usual ...h5 (to support ...g4) in the hope of playing ...⌁h5.

20 ⌁c7?! g3!

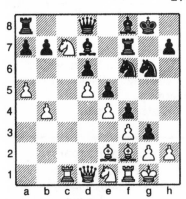

277

21 ⌁xa8? ⌁h5!

The young Dutch grandmaster has ignored Black's growing king-side threats to his peril! 22...Wh4 is threatened, and Piket's desperate attempts to defend are too late.

**22 ♔h1 gxf2 23 ♖xf2 ♘g3+!
24 ♔g1**

If 24 hxg3? fxg3 and Black's queen will swoop down to h2.

**24...♕xa8 25 ♗c4 a6! 26 ♕d3?!
♕a7 27 b5 axb5 28 ♗xb5**

278

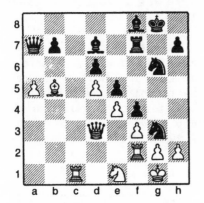

28...♘h1!

The final blow arrives from the queenside – Black will emerge a piece up.

White resigns.

Garry Kasparov –
Anatoly Karpov
*World Championship Match,
Lyons, France 1990*
Ruy Lopez

**1 e4 e5 2 ♘f3 ♘c6 3 ♗b5 a6 4
♗a4 ♘f6 5 0-0 ♗e7 6 ♖e1 b5 7
♗b3 d6 8 c3 0-0 9 h3**

Reaching the most popular opening position in chess history:
the main line of the Ruy Lopez. White's last move guards against ...♗g4 by Black and prepares to build a strong centre with pawns at e4 and d4. Kasparov and Karpov have played this variation many times in their 5(!) World Championship matches.

**9...♗b7 10 d4 ♖e8 11 ♘bd2
♗f8 12 a4 h6 13 ♗c2 exd4 14
cxd4 ♘b4 15 ♗b1 c5 16 d5 ♘d7
17 ♖a3 f5 18 ♖ae3 ♘f6 19 ♘h2
♔h8 20 b3!**

Preparing for the bishop to go to b2, controlling the long diagonal leading to the black king. White's pieces (particularly the bishops lurking on the queenside and the rooks doubled along the e-file) are excellently placed to begin a kingside attack. Karpov is trying to weaken the pawn at d5 by attacking the supporting e4-pawn and also hopes to use his extra queenside pawn. Whose strategy will succeed?

**20...bxa4 21 bxa4 c4 22 ♗b2
fxe4 23 ♘xe4 ♘fxd5 24 ♖g3
♖e6! 25 ♘g4 ♕e8** (see diagram 279)

26 ♘xh6!

Kasparov unleashes his forces against the defenders of the king with great power! Black, who has been defending very well up to now, elects not to capture the white knight at h6 with his rook (allowing 27 ♘xd6, unveiling a dangerous discovered attack on Black's queen). Karpov tries to defend by blocking out the bishop at b2, but

279

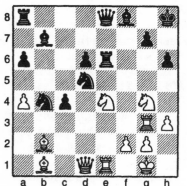

Kasparov's attack is simply too strong.

26...c3 27 ♘f5! cxb2 28 ♕g4 ♗c8 29 ♕h4+ ♖h6 30 ♘xh6 gxh6 31 ♔h2 ♕e5 32 ♘g5 ♕f6 33 ♖e8 ♗f5

280

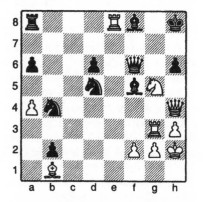

At this point – when both players had very little time to reach

the time-control at move 40 – Kasparov finds a winning queen sacrifice. Perhaps 34 ♘f7+! would have been even better, with a mating attack, but Kasparov takes a practical decision to force a winning endgame.

34 ♕xh6+! ♕xh6 35 ♘f7+ ♔h7 36 ♗xf5+ ♕g6 37 ♗xg6+ ♔g7 38 ♖xa8 ♗e7 39 ♖b8 a5 40 ♗e4+ ♔xf7 41 ♗xd5+ Black resigns.

Garry Kasparov –
Vishy Anand
Tilburg, Holland, 1991
Sicilian Defence

1 e4 c5 2 ♘f3 ♘c6 3 d4 cxd4 4 ♘xd4 ♕c7 5 ♘c3 e6 6 ♗e3 a6 7 ♗d3 ♘f6 8 0-0 ♘e5 9 h3 ♗c5 10 ♔h1 d6 11 f4 ♘c6?

The wrong square for the knight – blocking the queen's defence of the bishop on c5 in some crucial lines.

12 e5! (see diagram 281)

Ruthlessly exploiting Anand's opening slip, Kasparov smashes the centre open. If now 12...dxe5 then 13 ♘db5! axb5 14 ♗xc5 leaves Black's king very awkwardly stuck in the centre, so Vishy tries a different tack.

12...♘xe5 13 fxe5 dxe5 14 ♗b5+

By this ingenious device White finds a way into the d6 square for his knight. Another attacking idea aiming to blast a way through to

281

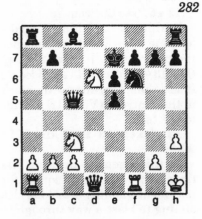

the black king, 14 ♘db5!, was found after the game to be even more convincing. Unfortunately for Anand, he now misses the best defence, 14...♔f8!, which would have put up significantly more resistance.

14...axb5? 15 ♘dxb5 ♕b6 16 ♗xc5 ♕xc5 17 ♘d6+ ♔e7

282

18 ♖xf6!
Removing a crucial defender. Kasparov's force of queen and two knights (with a rook ready in reserve) is more than a match for Black's "sleeping giants".
18...gxf6 19 ♘ce4 ♕d4 20 ♕h5 ♖f8 21 ♖d1! ♕e3 22 ♕h4 ♕f4 23 ♕e1!
Deftly swinging round to the queenside. Black's queen cannot cover all the angles as the two knights dominate the battlefield.
23...♖a4 24 ♕c3 ♖d4 25 ♖xd4 ♕f1+ 26 ♔h2 exd4 27 ♕c5 ♔d7 28 ♘b5 ♕f4+ 29 g3 Black resigns.

Anatoly Karpov – Garry Kasparov
Linares, Spain, 1993
King's Indian Defence

1 d4 ♘f6 2 c4 g6 3 ♘c3 ♗g7 4 e4 d6 5 f3 0-0 6 ♗e3 e5 7 ♘ge2 c6 8 ♕d2 ♘bd7 9 ♖d1 a6
A typical situation has arisen in the King's Indian Defence, where White is trying to establish an advantage in the centre and Black, having safely castled, is ready to attack White's central position. Karpov's 9th and 10th moves, put together, spell trouble; having left the king on e1 (rather than castling queenside) it is very dangerous to open up the centre.
10 dxe5? ♘xe5 11 b3 b5 12 cxb5 axb5 13 ♕xd6 ♘fd7 14 f4 b4!

283

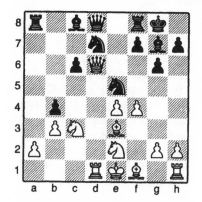

284

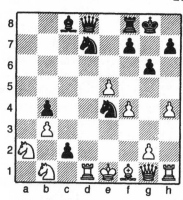

A surprise move, which Karpov had not seen. If the pawn is taken by 15 ♕xb4, Kasparov had prepared the remarkable combination 15...c5! 16 ♗xc5 ♘xc5! 17 ♖xd8 ♘ed3+ and Black wins back the queen with interest! The knight on c3, which had been holding White's position together, is forced to the edge of the board giving Kasparov very strong play.

15 ♘b1 ♘g4 16 ♗d4 ♗xd4 17 ♕xd4 ♖xa2 18 h3 c5 19 ♕g1 ♘gf6 20 e5 ♘e4 21 h4 What a sorry state the white pieces are in! Black's knight on e4 and rook on a2 dominate the position and it is high time for a breakthrough.

21...c4! 22 ♘c1 c3!?

Black has other ways to win, but this is certainly the most spectacular! The rook is sacrificed, but the humble c-pawn causes havoc amongst the white pieces.

23 ♘xa2 c2

White could try 24 ♖c1, but after 24...♘xe5! (playing directly for mate) 25 ♖xc2 ♗g4! 26 ♘d2 ♘d3+ Black's attack crashes through.

24 ♕d4? cxd1♕+ 25 ♔xd1 ♘dc5! 26 ♕xd8 ♖xd8+ 27 ♔c2 ♘f2

It's all over. The nicest finish would be 28 ♖g1 ♗f5+ 29 ♔b2 ♘d1+! 30 ♔a1 ♘xb3 mate.

White resigns.

Garry Kasparov –
Vladimir Kramnik
Novgorod, Russia, 1994
Sicilian Defence

1 e4 c5 2 ♘c3 ♘c6 3 ♘ge2 ♘f6 4 d4 cxd4 5 ♘xd4 e5 6 ♘db5 d6 7 ♗g5 a6 8 ♘a3 b5 9 ♘d5 ♗e7 10 ♗xf6 ♗xf6

Vladimir Kramnik is one of the most dangerous and talented "young pretenders" to Kasparov's crown, and had beaten Garry three times in 1994 before this game. Here he chooses the complex Sveshnikov variation of the Sicilian Defence, where Black gains the two bishops but allows White a strong outpost for his knight on d5. Those spectators who were expecting a "battle royal" were not to be disappointed ...!

11 c3 0-0 12 ♘c2 ♖b8 13 h4 ♘e7 14 ♘xf6+ gxf6 15 ♕d2

Black has allowed his kingside pawns to be weakened in return for getting rid of the strong d5-knight. With his last move Kasparov plans to castle queenside and launch a kingside attack. In a later game Garry preferred the strong 15 ♗d3!, keeping the option open for the queen to head to the kingside in one move by ♕h5.

15...♗b7 16 ♗d3 d5 17 exd5 ♕xd5 18 0-0-0 e4 19 ♗e2 ♕xa2 20 ♕h6 ♕e6 21 ♘d4 ♕b6 22 ♖h3 ♔h8 23 ♗g4 ♖g8 24 ♘e6!?

285

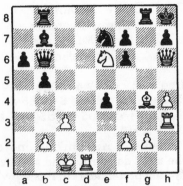

A quite surreal piece sacrifice! Capturing either knight or bishop is good for White: 24...fxe6 25 ♕xf6+ ♖g7 26 ♖d7; or 24...♖xg4 25 ♘g5! ♖xg5 26 hxg5 ♔g8 27 gxf6, and White wins.

24...♖g6 25 ♕f4 ♖e8?

By playing 25...♗d5! Kramnik could have repulsed the attack and questioned the correctness of Kasparov's imaginative play. Now, however, he is on the wrong end of a brilliant combination ...

26 ♖d6! ♘d5 27 h5!!

286

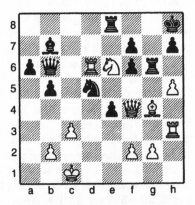

With both queens attacked in a truly complicated position, Garry simply gets on with attacking the enemy king! This game is a testament to the World Champion's imaginative attacking verve and fighting spirit.

27...♘xf4 28 hxg6 ♕xd6 29 ♖xh7+ ♔g8 30 gxf7+ ♔xh7 31 fxe8♕ ♘xe6 32 ♗f5+! ♔g7 33

♕g6+ ♔f8 34 ♕xf6+ ♔e8 35 ♗xe6 ♕f8?

After a long forcing sequence, Kramnik blunders (36 ♗d7+ wins the queen), but is in a clearly losing position anyway.

Black resigns.

Garry Kasparov –
Vishy Anand
*PCA World Championship
Match, New York, 1995*
Ruy Lopez

1 e4 e5 2 ♘f3 ♘c6 3 ♗b5 a6 4 ♗a4 ♘f6 5 0-0 ♘xe4

The Open Variation of the Ruy Lopez. The capture of White's central pawn generally leads to a complex, unbalanced position in which both sides have chances to play for a win. A run of eight drawn games in the match had been broken by Vishy Anand, who had beaten Kasparov's favourite Sicilian Defence in the ninth game. Garry was clearly out for revenge, and had a new idea hidden up his sleeve ...

6 d4 b5 7 ♗b3 d5 8 dxe5 ♗e6 9 ♘bd2 ♘c5 10 c3 d4 11 ♘g5

A piece sacrifice first played by Anatoly Karpov back in 1978. White's idea is 11...♕xg5 12 ♕f3, and it's not so easy for Black to counter the pin on the c6-knight.

11...dxc3 12 ♘xe6 fxe6 13 bxc3 ♕d3 14 ♗c2!

This is the start of Kasparov's incredible idea – involving the sacrifice of a whole rook! – worked out in the days before this game took place. Such deep preparation (Garry was moving almost instantaneously up to move 19, following home analysis!) has become his trademark.

14...♕xc3 15 ♘b3! ♘xb3 16 ♗xb3

287

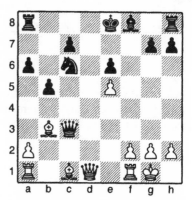

Inviting Anand to take the rook. After much thought Vishy decides against 16...♕xa1, which would be met by 17 ♕h5+ g6 18 ♕f3, and it is virtually impossible to meet the various threats – ♕xc6+, ♗xe6, ♕f6 as well as a deadly discovered attack on the queen when the bishop moves from c1.

16...♘d4 17 ♕g4 ♕xa1

Anand takes the rook anyway, but the onslaught from the white queen and two bishops is too powerful.

18 ♗xe6 ♖d8 19 ♗h6!

288

A devastating blow! White's attack breaks through to g7, when the black king's days are numbered. If 19...♕xf1+ 20 ♔xf1 gxh6 then mate follows with 21 ♕h5+ and 22 ♕f7, so Anand has no option but to bail out into an endgame a pawn down.

19...♕c3 20 ♗xg7 ♕d3 21 ♗xh8 ♕g6 22 ♗f6 ♗e7 23 ♗xe7 ♕xg4 24 ♗xg4 ♔xe7 25 ♖c1!

Kasparov shows excellent technique in converting the advantage of the extra pawn. Carefully restraining the Black queenside pawns, Garry prepares the advance of his own passed pawns, which will be decisive.

25...c6 26 f4 a5 27 ♔f2 a4 28 ♔e3 b4 29 ♗d1 a3 30 g4 ♖d5 31 ♖c4 c5 32 ♔e4 ♖d8 33 ♖xc5 ♘e6 34 ♖d5 ♖c8 35 f5 ♖c4+ 36 ♔e3 ♘c5 37 g5 ♖c1 38 ♖d6 **Black resigns.**

CPSIA information can be obtained
at www.ICGtesting.com
Printed in the USA
BVHW031706150919
558014BV00004B/8/P